Endorsements

Peg Arnold is an amazing creative for the Lord. It is no surprise that she is writing this book to help other creatives, such as speakers, sharpen their message by making it more memorable using the prop ideas she and others have given. It's exciting to see a community come together and make a project shine like this book, *Making Your Message Memorable: Creative Ideas for Captivating Presentations.*

Understanding the importance of diversity in learning is crucial. That alone speaks to creatives in honing their message so that it is ready to be received by the masses. God gifts us with many daily things that we can use. Being aware of these is crucial to delivering a message. Isn't that what Jesus did?

This is hands-on training. The workbook style helps the reader apply what they are learning to their message-giving ministry. You'll love it!

—Kathy Bruins, Founder of The Well Ministry for Creatives, Award-winning Author, and Speaker

I am thrilled to recommend Peg Arnold's insightful and resourceful book, *Making Your Message Memorable: Creative Ideas for Captivating Presentations.* This invaluable guide is a must-have for speakers, teachers, preachers, leaders, and writers who aspire to enhance their communication skills and leave a lasting impact on their audience.

Peg masterfully combines practical advice with creative strategies, making this book an essential tool for anyone looking to captivate their audience and deliver memorable messages. Her experience shines through each page, providing readers with a wealth of techniques to engage listeners, foster connection, and communicate with clarity and passion.

Whether you are a seasoned communicator or just beginning your journey, *Making Your Message Memorable* offers something for everyone. Peg's innovative ideas and proven methods will inspire you to elevate your presentations and ensure that your messages resonate long after they are delivered. This book is not only a treasure trove of knowledge but also a testament to Peg Arnold's dedication to empowering communicators of all kinds.

I highly recommend *Making Your Message Memorable* to anyone seeking to transform their presentations and leave a meaningful impression on their audience. Peg Arnold's wisdom and creativity will undoubtedly help you take your communication skills to the next level.

—Cindy Bultema, Speaker and Author of *Live Full, Walk Free* and *Red Hot Faith*

Peg Arnold's *Making Your Message Memorable* is a must-have resource for every speaker, teacher, or preacher looking to captivate their audience with creative, impactful ideas. Built on the foundation of learning styles, this book confirms that object lessons and visual aids significantly enhance how people remember and experience messages. Peg provides a treasure trove of innovative strategies and practical tools that are simple to learn and use. They will transform your presentations, devotions, and lessons into unforgettable experiences. Whether you're a seasoned speaker or just starting, this resource is essential for making your message not just heard, but truly remembered.

—Robyn Dykstra, National Speaker, Author, Professional Speaking Coach

Clever. Appealing. Engaging. Gripping. Exciting. These words describe the way master teacher Peg Arnold holds the attention of a classroom or an auditorium filled with conference participants. She's the educator we wish every student could have. As a speaker-trainer, I highly recommend this book, which is filled with poignant ways to capture the attention of your target audience and make Truth memorable. Peg is generous with ideas that will make your presentations unforgettable. *Making Your Message Memorable* is a timeless resource for speakers, teachers, writers, and leaders.

—Carol Kent, Founder and Executive Director of Speak Up Ministries, Speaker and Author
of *Speak Up with Confidence* (NavPress)

Making Your Message Memorable is a treasure trove for every type of speaker! Peg Arnold shares illustrations, ideas, and props to captivate your audience. They will walk away with a better understanding of your message and likely never forget it. Peg also shares tips every speaker needs to help craft and deliver a better message. If you're a speaker, you need this book!

—Andrea Lende, Best-Selling Author, Speaker, and CEO of Beatitudes Publishing LLC

This book is an absolute must-read for ministers, speakers, and trainers doing ministry work. *Making Your Message Memorable* by Peg Arnold ignited my creative juices for future sermons and speaking engagements. Her insight resonated with me as a speaker, parent, and educator who depends on communication to move people forward. With over 100 practical and creative ideas to bring one's message to life, this book equips us with the tools to empower our audiences for transformational impact.

—Ed Reed, Minister, Global Leadership Trainer & Keynote Speaker

Jesus utilized illustrations and stories to convey his transformational teachings, so it only makes sense that we would do the same. As a pastor, I am always looking for fresh ways to make the Scripture engaging and memorable, so this book is a great resource. Thank you, Peg, for compiling this treasure trove and modeling creative communication so well.

—Aaron Stern, Lead Pastor of Mill City Church and Author of *What's Your Secret?*

From pedagogue to creativity and research to delivery, Peg Arnold's vast speaking and teaching experience, combined with her dramatic flair, provides the perfect tips to take your speaking to the next level. *Making Your Message Memorable* is easy to read and well organized. You'll especially love the section with over 90 props and ideas. Don't just stand there and talk; become unforgettable!

—Marnie Swedberg, International Speaker and Author of Fourteen Books

Peg Arnold has a gift for teaching. Her creative use of everyday objects and dramatic presentations engage the audience in a place where understanding and transformation will be evident. Her book *Making Your Message Memorable* is a valuable resource for any speaker as it gives ideas for their message and walks them through how to study the text accurately. In a workshop, Peg teaches practical teaching techniques to make any message come alive. Anyone looking for a fresh way to present their message will walk away with effective ideas to use the next time they speak.

—Carol Tetzlaff, Redemption Press

Peg Arnold is a master storyteller! Her messages last years in the minds of all who hear her speak. She has the gift of keeping audiences engaged and on the edge of their seats.

—Tammy Whitehurst, Speaker and Writer

Making Your Message Memorable

Creative Ideas for Captivating Presentations

Making Your Message Memorable
Copyright © 2024 Peg Arnold.
ISBN: 978-1-963377-22-4 (spiral bound)
ISBN: 978-1-963377-42-2 (paperback)

Published by Abundance Books, LLC, Kalamazoo, MI
abundance-books.com

Interior design by Michelle Kenny
Cover design by Michelle Kenny

10 9 8 7 6 5 4 3 2 1

Scripture taken from THE HOLY BIBLE, NEW INTERNATIONAL VERSION ®.
Copyright© 1973, 1978, 1984, 2011 by Biblica, Inc.™. Used by permission of Zondervan

All vector graphics are courtesy of Pixabay.com unless otherwise noted.
All charts and graphs are created by the author.

Disclaimer
This book is a collection of specific ideas to enrich your message. It is not intended to cover
every possibility but to provide a springboard for creativity. Inside, you'll discover insights
from the authors' and contributors' experiences, all meant to enhance your ministry
with visuals and props. Though you may spot some familiar concepts, diligent effort has
been made to credit sources. Remember, these resources are provided to add depth and
engagement to your message, especially when paired with prayer and practice.

Making Your Message Memorable

Creative Ideas for Captivating Presentations

A Resource for Speakers, Teachers, Preachers, Leaders, and Writers

PEG ARNOLD

Table of Contents

Introduction

Can you recall a message that moved or captivated you? What made it memorable? Growing up as a PK (preacher's kid), I still remember one of my father's sermons from elementary school. When I entered the sanctuary, a water-filled fishbowl beside the pulpit caught my attention. My father mesmerized me as he turned the water dark with dye. Then, the water magically became clear as he explained the impact of Christ's forgiveness of our sins. (See Ephesians 1:7 entry, page 78.)

Ten years later, as a teacher, I hoped to have a similar impact on others. I was fascinated by the concept of different learning styles and the brain's developmental stages. I discovered that physical props engage the brain differently than verbal communication, increasing retention for the listener. This inspired me to integrate props into my oral reports and lessons when I returned to college. I even created a pyramid of red blocks to guide the presentation of a collegiate-level research project. That professor invited me to speak to her Intro to Counseling class three years later.

Now I understand why Jesus taught spiritual concepts using object lessons, analogies, and parables. He knew how visuals engaged the brain differently than verbal communication, increasing retention for the listener. Wouldn't I want to do the same for my lessons and messages?

Paul even uses the body as a word picture describing the value of different gifts and abilities in the church at Corinth.

"Just as a body, though one, has many parts, but all its many parts form one body, so it is with Christ... The eye cannot say to the hand, "I don't need you!" And the head cannot say to the feet, 'I don't need you!' On the contrary, those parts of the body that seem to be weaker are indispensable" (1 Corinthians 12:12, 21-22).

Whether incorporating visual aids is a new concept for you or you already recognize their power, this resource is designed for you. First, we will explore research that supports the use of visual aids. The rest of the book equips you with more than ninety creative, scripture-based visual aids and techniques. Each one is aimed to capture attention, trigger emotion, and improve retention.

Chapter 1: Exploring Communication

Visuals engage the mind, ease understanding, and are most remembered.
—John Medina

ﷻ

I had always wanted to be a teacher. As a little girl, I lined up my dolls and stuffed animals as students and presented lessons to them. I started my educational career teaching math, reading, and music. That first year, I was overwhelmed while learning the value of discipline, communication, and preparation. In my lessons, I tried implementing various methods of presenting information, including visual models with oral instructions.

I saw a significant increase in student engagement when I used physical objects and images. This led me to explore Gardner's multiple intelligences theory. He researched different ways humans process information and learn.[1] This influenced how I taught as I tried to integrate different strategies into my lessons to positively impact student retention. I had them complete assessments so they could discover more about the various ways to learn. Howard Gardner's areas of intelligence include:

1. Visual-spatial
2. Linguistic-verbal
3. Logical-mathematical
4. Body-kinesthetic
5. Musical
6. Interpersonal
7. Intrapersonal
8. Naturalistic

Over the years, I have taught various subjects and age groups and spoken at conferences. Regardless of the age or setting, I utilize multiple presentation methods, including visual aids, group discussions, oral presentations, drama, and physical movement. It never ceases to amaze me when someone seeks to thank me for including visuals in my presentation after an event.

A recent attendee replied, "I am so glad you use props! I am a visual learner, and this kept my attention. I will remember your message."

As a speaker, teacher, or presenter, discovering the approach that best suits your personality and intended audience is critical to an effective and powerful message. Integrating visual aids, descriptive stories, and colorful presentations goes beyond aesthetics because it captures attention and engages different portions of the brain. This practice is called the multimodal learning (MML) process. Most messages and lessons are presented orally, but the MML process engages at least two or more activities to help communicate the concept.[1] This does not negate Gardner's research but builds upon it.

---

[1] Howard Gardner. *Intelligence Reframed: Multiple Intelligences for the 21st Century* (New York: Basic Books, 1999)

Communicating the Message

There are five ways in which messages are communicated. The multimodal model combines the senses and the learning modalities to define these five approaches:

1. Linguistic: words
2. Aural: sounds
3. Gestures: body language
4. Visual: images[2]
5. Spatial: physical arrangements

Richard Mayer, author of *Multimedia Learning*, discovered that when a presentation combines two or more of the above communication modalities, the understanding and retention of the information improves by 50-75%.[3]

Have you ever watched gifted storytellers? They combine several of the communication modalities listed above, including facial expressions, voice inflections, and body movements, to express emotions and create images that engage the senses and captivate the listener. Throughout most of this book, you will discover additional ways props can increase listener engagement.

Receiving the Message

God created humans with five senses—hearing, touch, smell, taste, and sight—to interpret the world. Communication generally uses two senses: hearing and sight.

Dr. Albert Mehrabian explores these two modalities in his communication model. His research suggests that people receive messages more through body language and tone of voice:

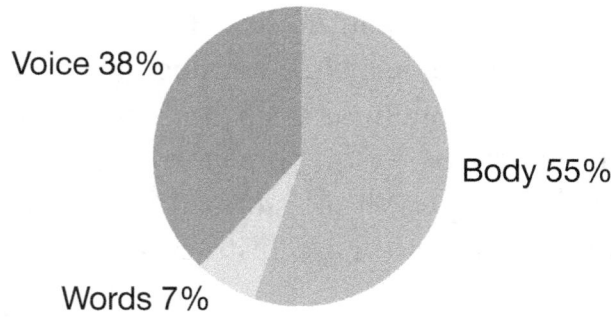

- 7% through words—the actual words we are speaking.

- 55% through body language—our body's visual and physical actions, including facial expressions.

- 38% through vocal inflections—our voice's pitch, pace, tone, and volume.[4]

These percentages apply more to face-to-face interactions. It amazes me how much is communicated nonverbally.

---

[2] Alison Yang, "Multiliteracies Through Multimodal Teaching," *Building Learning Agility*, February 18, 2022, https://alisonyang.com/multimodal-teaching/.

[2] Yang, "Multiliteracies."

[3] Richard Mayer and Roxana Moreno, "A Cognitive Theory of Multimedia Learning: Implications for Design Principles," *Research Gate*, January 2005, https://www.researchgate.net/publication/248528255_A_Cognitive_Theory_of_Multimedia_Learning_Implications_for_Design_Principles.

[4] Albert Mehrabian and Susan R. Ferris, "Inference of Attitudes from Nonverbal Communication in Two Channels," *Journal of Consulting Psychology* 31, no. 3 (1967): 249–52, https://doi.org/10.1037/h0024648.

Learning modalities are how a person processes, accumulates, and retains information. The three main types of learners are:

1. Visual—Learning through sight.

2. Auditory—Learning through listening.

3. Kinesthetic—Learning through movement.

In the general population, 65% are visual learners, 30% are auditory learners, and 5% are kinesthetic learners.[5]

The Three Types of Learners

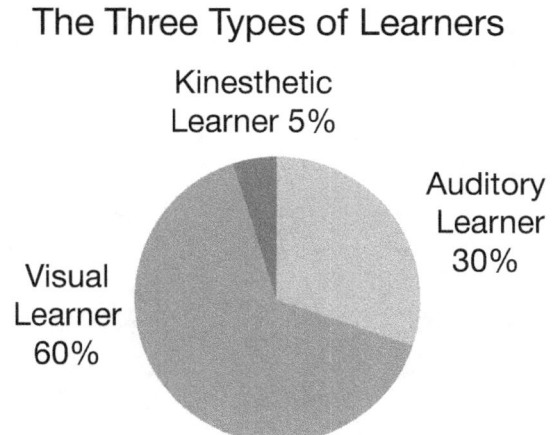

Kinesthetic Learner 5%

Auditory Learner 30%

Visual Learner 60%

Embracing God's Creativity

Why is it important to know how people receive information and learn? Because when we understand how people learn, we can incorporate modalities in our teaching that resonate with our audience. God designed people with unique learning styles and uses each of us to share our messages in distinctively different methods (1 Corinthians 12:12).

Jesus understood the power of visuals in communication. He engaged His audiences by creating word pictures and analogies that used everyday elements and events. He communicated profound truths to a broad audience by incorporating familiar cultural images, such as fig trees, sheep, rocks, soil types, and water. As followers of Jesus, shouldn't we strive to teach like He did? After all, isn't it our goal to deliver God's truth in understandable ways?

Conclusion

Knowing that 55% of communication is conveyed through body language and 65% of individuals are visual learners highlights the importance of incorporating visual aids to enhance your message. So, don't be shy about embracing visual aids; they'll make your communication more effective, helping your message stick and keep your audience engaged.

---

[5]Mark Moss, "A Recruiters Guide To Connect With Job Candidates And Clients," Call Logic, March 31, 2021, https://www.calllogic.com/?s=A+Recruiters+Guide+To+Connect+With+Job+Candidates+And+Clients.

Chapter 2: Researching the Facts

Visual communication has more power than mere words.
—Jock Kinneir

Earlier, I shared some facts from Richard Mayer, who conducted extensive cognitive research with students using written and verbal instructions. After three days of oral-only lessons, students could recall only 10% of what they heard. The retention rate jumped to over 35% if a visual display accompanied the lesson. Therefore, integrating visuals increased retention by 350%![6]

In my twenty-five years of teaching and counseling, I have experienced the impact of using visuals and manipulatives to improve student learning. I witnessed an increase in my students' achievement and their knowledge retention. I firmly believe in the effectiveness of this multimodal model and have designed and taught courses on these concepts to many others.

Here are six advantages of integrating visuals into your message or lesson:

1. **Visuals create curiosity and grab attention.**

   Has your curiosity ever been piqued when you see flowers, shoes, or water pitchers decorating the front of the room? Often, I receive questions about the displayed items before speaking.

   One time, an older man saw the collection of shoes and boots stacked on shelves next to the lectern and gruffly asked, "Are we having a yard sale today?"

   I smiled and responded, "I know it does look odd, but I guarantee there's a message in there somewhere."

   Upon leaving the church that morning, he shook my hand and said, "Now that's a sermon I'll remember!"

2. **Visuals activate the long-term memory part of the brain.**

   Listening to words and seeing something simultaneously activates two parts of our brain, improving our focus and comprehension. Using two parts of our brain exemplifies the multimodal learning model. I met two women at a wedding last year. They came up to me and asked if I was Peg Arnold. I nodded and asked why.

   "You spoke about Mary and Martha at our women's retreat seven years ago. We still remember that message!" I integrated

[6]Richard E. Mayer and Roxana Moreno, *"A Cognitive Theory of Multimedia Learning: Implications for Design Principles,"* Research Gate, January 2005, https://www.researchgate.net/publication/248528255_A_Cognitive_Theory_of_Multimedia_Learning_Implications_for_Design_Principles.

drama, visual props, group discussions, posters, and charts into the messages and activities at that retreat.

3. Visuals make abstract and complex ideas more concrete and easier to understand.

As a middle school counselor, I spent years sharing the power of personifying metaphors through visual aids. Props help to simplify or make the concept come alive for the student.[7]

For example, I had a student break a pencil to understand the impact of lying to her mom. We discussed how trust is like a bridge of connection. The broken pencil symbolizes how that trust was broken by her lying. As we taped the two parts together, I explained that, like a broken bone, the trust bond would heal, but it would take time. Even though the pencil will not repair itself, it gave the student a concrete metaphor for the situation. We listed positive actions she could take to strengthen the relationship with her mom. Three weeks later, she met with me, discussed the changes she had made, and reported that things were better. She pulled the taped pencil out of her pocket, saying, "I keep this as my reminder."

4. Visuals trigger emotions.

Frederick Barnard said a picture is worth 1,000 words. Just the right image can evoke emotions. It could be a photograph, an image on a slide, or a physical prop.

One of the most impressive visual aids I have seen is a broken pot (see page 22). An image can also be brought to life by weaving the five senses into the details of a well-told story.

Props can help you when you write. Try placing the specific object next to your computer while describing it. You may be surprised how this approach stimulates your brain and enhances your descriptions and details.

5. Visual aids with color increase interest and improve focus and memory.[8]

This is an effective marketing strategy used in many advertisements. The last time I copied materials at a Staples office store, one of the copier's screens displayed this fact.

6. Visual aids and props can help keep a message organized.

Every new object or differentiated use of an object can be used as a memory trigger for the speaker, reengaging the audience. I often line up my props in the order of my outline. This allows me to focus on the message and audience rather than my notes.

---

[7] J. Lockard and J. R. Sidowski, "Learning in Fourth and Sixth Graders as a Function of Sensory Mode of Stimulus Presentation and Overt or Covert Practice," Journal of Educational Psychology 52 (October 1961): 262-65.

[8] Mariam Adawiah Dzulkifli and Muhammad Faiz Mustafar, "The Influence of Colour on Memory Performance: A Review," Malaysian Journal of Medical Sciences 20, no. 2 (March 2013): 3–9, https://www.ncbi.nlm.nih.gov/pmc/articles/PMC3743993/.

Chapter 3: Bringing Scripture to Life

Visual Aids for Specific Scriptures

The following section provides various resources, visual aids, and props specifically designed to be used with the identified scriptures. They are organized in chronological order, as found in the Bible.

Each verse reference includes

1. a theme
2. visual aid(s)
3. an application description
4. reflection prompts

Providing just the scripture reference lets you choose your preferred translation. These ideas can be incorporated as an introduction, opening story, or guide your overall message. Feel free to modify the concept, but remember, never manipulate the scripture out of context to fit your lesson.

There are many repeated themes throughout the Bible; thus, some of the visual aids in this book apply to more scriptures than the ones listed. You may choose to use the one listed or adapt the idea to one of your own. The author provided duplicate themes and visual aids to demonstrate this option.

The application is kept elementary, allowing you to expand the message with your testimony and story based on this illustration, making it more personal, powerful, and significant. Various Christian speakers and preachers have contributed some of these ideas. Their name is at the bottom of the selection, and their contact information is at the back of the book. If no contributor is cited, it is an idea the author has used in her ministry.

Integrating props into a message requires preparation:

- gathering the items
- deciding how to demonstrate the concept
- practicing your message with the props
- choosing how to display them at the venue

You can find additional preparation ideas in Chapter 6: Delivery and Preparation.

The visual aids listed are suggested props. If you cannot locate the items, using a picture instead of physical objects is always an option. However, research[9] supports the idea that using three-dimensional objects, compared to two-dimensional images, can significantly impact the message because the brain processes them differently. As you prepare your message for a specific audience, pray, use the reflection prompts to guide you, and seek the Lord's direction at every step.

---

[9] Jacqueline C. Snow, Rafal M. Skiba, Taylor L. Coleman, and Marian E. Berryhill, "Real-World Objects Are More Memorable Than Photographs of Objects," *Frontiers in Human Neuroscience* 8 (October 19, 2014), https://doi.org/10.3389/fnhum.2014.00837.

Bringing Scripture to Life

❦

Visual Aids for Old Testament

Visual aids are the most universal language in the world.
—Rudolph Arnheim

1. Scripture: Exodus 14:13–31

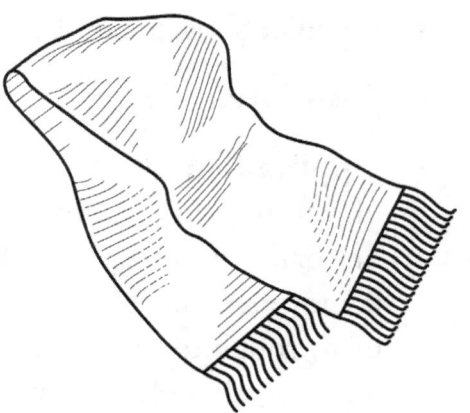

- **Theme:** Trust God—Moses Leads the Israelites Across the Red Sea

- **Visual Aids:** Use blue cloth at least seven feet long and a long stick to be used as a staff.

- **Application:** Have someone help you hold up the cloth to represent the wall of seawater. Describe the scene and the difficulties trying to cross the sea. Hold up the staff as Moses might have, then drop the cloth to represent the water parting and the miracle God performed to save the Israelites. Lift the cloth back up again to stop the Egyptians.

Read the entire chapter that contains this passage. Reflect and pray about its meaning. _____

_____

- What insights are there when considering the historical or situational context? _____

_____

- What speaks to you directly? _____

_____

- How does it apply to your message? _____

_____

- What personal story will you describe to help others apply this truth?_____

_____

_____

- What type of preparation might you need to use the props effectively? _____

_____

2. Scripture: Exodus 20:3

- **Theme:** Should God Be First?

- **Visual Aid:** Use a bike wheel.

- **Application:** We are told that God should be the center of our lives, like the hub of a bicycle wheel, rather than one of the wheel's spokes. When God is one of the spokes, it indicates that He is just a part of our lives, allowing us to rotate to other things. What is holding the wheel together, though? When God is the center, everything is dependent on Him. Each spoke depends on the center; take out the center, and the wheel is inoperable. What happens when God is not the center of our lives?

- **Contributor:** Aaron Stern

Read the entire chapter that contains this passage. Reflect and pray about its meaning. _____

_____

- What insights are there when considering the historical or situational context? _____

_____

- What speaks to you directly? _____

_____

- How does it apply to your message? _____

_____

- What personal story will you describe to help others apply this truth?_____

_____

- What type of preparation might you need to use the props effectively? _____

_____

3. Scripture: Leviticus 19:9–11

- **Theme:** Stress

- **Visual Aids:** Use dominoes.

- **Application:** Line up the dominoes as you name the stresses and distractions that don't allow margin. Lack of margin can be described as having a tight schedule, putting too many activities on the schedule. Give examples. Show how one unexpected move knocks them down. Then, space the dominoes farther apart explaining the concept of margin, and how to reprioritize your activities. When the dominoes are farther apart, pushing one down doesn't knock them all down.

Read the entire chapter that contains this passage. Reflect and pray about its meaning. _____

_____

- What insights are there when considering the historical or situational context? _____

_____

- What speaks to you directly? _____

_____

- How does it apply to your message? _____

_____

- What personal story will you describe to help others apply this truth?_____

_____

- What type of preparation might you need to use the props effectively? _____

_____

4. Scripture: Leviticus 27:30

Additional Scripture Resource: ***Deuteronomy 14:22***

- **Theme:** Tithing

- **Visual Aids:** Gather ten to twenty matching pieces of at least six different small items, such as Hershey's Kisses, quarters, and small trinkets. You will also need one small vase and one large vase.

- **Application:** Explain the meaning of a tithe. Bring out each set of items, count them, and create piles of 18 items and two items. Explain that a tithe is 10%. 10% of twenty is two. Put the two items of each group into the small vase. Then, pour the remainder (the 18 items) into the large vase. Repeat this with each set of items. Hold up each vase when finished; the visual of the difference is striking and can be life changing.

> I used this in a children's sermon. Afterwards, many adults commented on the power of seeing this example—so much so that they were prayerfully considering changing their giving habits.

Read the entire chapter that contains this passage. Reflect and pray about its meaning. _____

_____

- What insights are there when considering the historical or situational context? _____

_____

- What speaks to you directly? _____

_____

- How does it apply to your message? _____

_____

- What personal story will you describe to help others apply this truth?_____

_____

- What type of preparation might you need to use the props effectively? _____

_____

5. Scripture: Joshua 4:1–7

- **Theme:** Stones of Remembrance: Creating a Legacy

- **Visual Aids:** Collect five to seven stones. Pass around the stones or display large stones if on a stage. Discuss the story and the reason for the stones. The stones were a reminder to the future generations of God's works and faithfulness.

- **Application:** What are some "stones of remembrance" others have left for you? What stones of remembrance are you leaving for others? (Sometimes, I bring some of my family remembrances, such as a quilt, a recipe, a book, and so on).

> A wonderful follow-up activity to this message is to hand out index cards. Have the participants share a meaningful stone of remembrance in their lives with a partner, then write a legacy they hope to leave and a possible symbol for it on the index card.

Read the entire chapter that contains this passage. Reflect and pray about its meaning. _____

_____

- What insights are there when considering the historical or situational context? _____

_____

- What speaks to you directly? _____

_____

- How does it apply to your message? _____

_____

- What personal story will you describe to help others apply this truth?_____

_____

_____

- What type of preparation might you need to use the props effectively? _____

_____

6. Scripture: Ruth 1

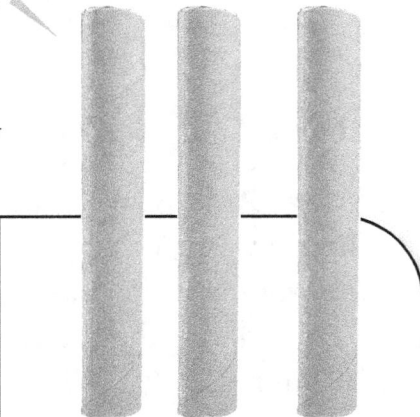

- **Theme:** Telling the Story of Naomi's Family: from Great Joy to Significant Loss

- **Visual Aids:** Use three toilet paper rolls to represent the women in this story and three paper towel rolls to represent the men. Choose three colors for the toilet paper rolls and use the same ones for the paper towel rolls.

- **Application:** The tall rolls are the men, and the shorter rolls are the women. Introduce Naomi and Elimelech, choosing a matching-colored pair of rolls. Then, introduce their sons, using the paper towel rolls. Finally, introduce their wives, Orpah and Ruth. Match the colors for each pair. Describe this beautiful family of six. Then, as you recall the story, remove the rolls representing the family members who die or return home. This leaves only Ruth and Naomi. This visual is powerful as it magnifies Naomi's extreme loss. Be sure to highlight God's faithfulness in the relationship with Boaz.

> I used this visual for a Sunday morning sermon. Afterward, several people mentioned its impact.

Read the entire chapter that contains this passage. Reflect and pray about its meaning. _____

_____

- What insights are there when considering the historical or situational context? _____

_____

- What speaks to you directly? _____

_____

- How does it apply to your message? _____

_____

- What personal story will you describe to help others apply this truth?_____

_____

- What type of preparation might you need to use the props effectively? _____

_____

7. Scripture: 1 Samuel 16:7

Idea One

- **Theme:** Telling the Story Behind the Faces

- **Visual Aid:** Use a picture of your family.

- **Application:** Pictures always show the best side of us. Post the picture and share each family member's real story including struggles and joys. Make sure you have permission. This same concept can be used when telling your story. Display pictures of yourself at each stage of your journey.

When I saw Jill present this at the Speak Up conference, it was so powerful that I still remember her message today.

- **Contributor:** Jill Savage

Read the entire chapter that contains this passage. Reflect and pray about its meaning. _____

_____

- What insights are there when considering the historical or situational context? _____

_____

- What speaks to you directly? _____

_____

- How does it apply to your message? _____

_____

- What personal story will you describe to help others apply this truth?_____

_____

_____

- What type of preparation might you need to use the props effectively? _____

_____

_____

8. *Scripture: 1 Samuel 16:7*

Idea Two

Image: vecteezy.com

- **Theme:** Man Sees the Outside, but God Looks at the Heart.

- **Visual Aids:** Use five to seven wrapped boxes and gift bags. Wrap the outside to significantly contrast with the inside. (For example, use plain wrapping paper and place a precious jewel inside, or use beautiful wrapping paper and place broken pieces inside.)

- **Application:** If there is time, have volunteers come up and take a gift, predict what might be inside, open it, and give their first thoughts and impressions. Describe how we see the outside, but God sees the heart. Describe how many of us protect our inner hurts, shame, and fears with an incongruent appearance. Share your personal story and remind them that nothing is hidden from our loving God.

Read the entire chapter that contains this passage. Reflect and pray about its meaning. _____

_____

- What insights are there when considering the historical or situational context? _____

_____

- What speaks to you directly? _____

_____

- How does it apply to your message? _____

_____

- What personal story will you describe to help others apply this truth?_____

_____

_____

- What type of preparation might you need to use the props effectively? _____

_____

9. Scripture: Psalm 30:8–12

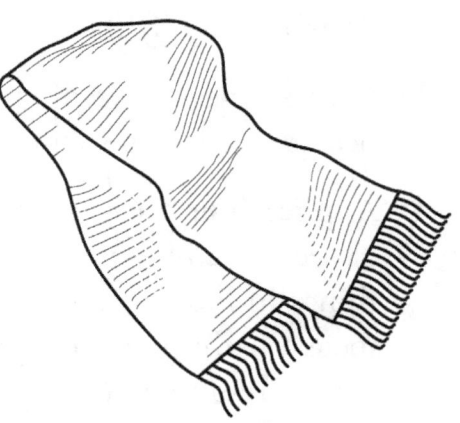

- **Theme:** Depression

- **Visual Aid:** Use a dark, solid-colored scarf.

- **Application:** Place this scarf over your head or around your body like a shawl as you read verses 8-10. (Vary your voice and body language to match the mood.) This visually emphasizes the difficulty of the situation. As you read verses 11-12 and describe God's faithfulness in your story, remove the scarf and hold it up like a cape or wings to symbolize your newfound freedom.

Read the entire chapter that contains this passage. Reflect and pray about its meaning. _____

_____

- What insights are there when considering the historical or situational context? _____

_____

- What speaks to you directly? _____

_____

- How does it apply to your message? _____

_____

- What personal story will you describe to help others apply this truth?_____

_____

_____

- What type of preparation might you need to use the props effectively? _____

_____

10. Scripture: Psalm 34:3

- **Theme:** Magnify the Lord

- **Visual Aids:** Use reading glasses, a magnifying glass, binoculars, a telescope, and a microscope.

- **Application:** Each of these magnifies and/or allows us to see something more clearly. Do we magnify the little things in life that can cause stress and anxiety, or do we focus on the Lord and magnify our perception of His nature, resulting in His peace?

- **Contributor:** Emma Kelln

Image: vecteezy.com

Read the entire chapter that contains this passage. Reflect and pray about its meaning. _____

_____

- What insights are there when considering the historical or situational context? _____

_____

- What speaks to you directly? _____

_____

- How does it apply to your message? _____

_____

- What personal story will you describe to help others apply this truth?_____

_____

_____

- What type of preparation might you need to use the props effectively? _____

_____

_____

11. *Scripture: Psalm 34:18*

- **Theme:** Brokenness and Healing

- **Visual Aids:** Use broken pottery or broken ceramic cups, pictures of mosaics, and pottery that the kintsugi process has repaired.

- **Application:** Difficult experiences may have broken us, but God heals us. Our vessel may not look the same, but He repurposes us. Kintsugi is a Japanese art form that glues the pieces back together with precious metals, making the vessel stronger and more beautiful. Another way God brings purpose to brokenness is by redesigning us into a new creation. A mosaic picture or a stained-glass window is another way of demonstrating God creating beauty from brokenness since it is constructed from broken pieces.

> I received a note from a woman who took a picture of these images. She had never considered that God was creating something new from her brokenness and loss. Instead of being stuck in the past, she was embracing the possibilities.

Read the entire chapter that contains this passage. Reflect and pray about its meaning. _____

_____

- What insights are there when considering the historical or situational context? _____

_____

- What speaks to you directly? _____

_____

- How does it apply to your message? _____

_____

- What personal story will you describe to help others apply this truth?_____

_____

_____

- What type of preparation might you need to use the props effectively? _____

_____

12. *Scripture: Psalm 34:18*   *Idea Two*

- **Theme:** Broken to Beautiful

- **Visual Aids:** Use broken pottery that has been glued back together with pieces missing. Include a battery-operated light inside.

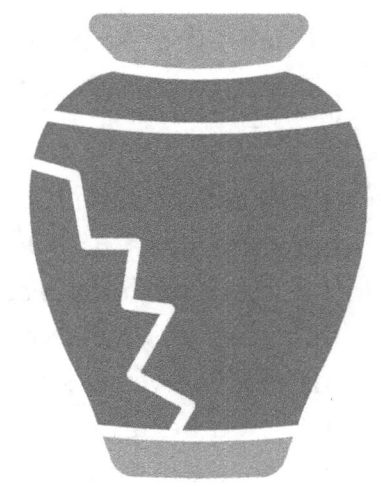

- **Application:** Difficult experiences can make us feel broken. Hold up the clay pot, broken and glued back together, for the audience to see. Point out the beauty of the light shining through the cracks. This illustration of light glistening its way through the cracks in the clay pot gives hope and beauty to our broken places.[10]

- **Contributor:** Jodi Snowdon

Image: vecteezy.com

Read the entire chapter that contains this passage. Reflect and pray about its meaning. _____

_____

- What insights are there when considering the historical or situational context? _____

_____

- What speaks to you directly? _____

_____

- How does it apply to your message? _____

_____

- What personal story will you describe to help others apply this truth?_____

_____

_____

- What type of preparation might you need to use the props effectively? _____

_____

[10]Patsy Clairmont, *God Uses Cracked Pots* (Carol Stream, IL: Focus on the Family, 1991).

13. Scripture: Psalm 37:5

*Additional Scripture Resource: **Matthew 6:33***

- **Theme:** Priorities

- **Visual Aids:** Use a large jar, marshmallows (large and small), and rice. You can also use two sizes of rocks or shells with sand.

- **Application:** The largest item represents your priorities. When we start filling our life (the jar) with our priorities (God, family, and friends), there is room for everything else. Fill the rest of the jar with rice. Then, demonstrate assembling it in the opposite order. If you try putting in the "fluff" of life (rice or sand) first, the marshmallows won't fit; they get squished out.[11]

- **Contributor:** Kris Howsley King

Image: vecteezy.com

Read the entire chapter that contains this passage. Reflect and pray about its meaning. _____

_____

- What insights are there when considering the historical or situational context? _____

_____

- What speaks to you directly? _____

_____

- How does it apply to your message? _____

_____

- What personal story will you describe to help others apply this truth?_____

_____

_____

- What type of preparation might you need to use the props effectively? _____

_____

[11] Jeremy Wright, "Time Management: The Pickle Jar Theory," A List Apart, June 22, 2002, https://alistapart.com/article/pickle/.

14. Scripture: Psalm 51:7

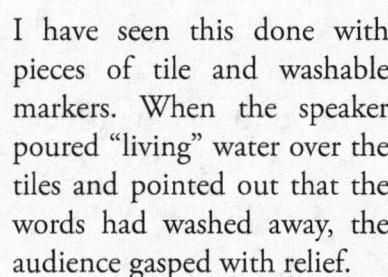

- **Theme:** Washing Away Sins

- **Visual Aids:** Place a large, clear bowl filled with water at the front. Rest a pottery pitcher beside it. Have index cards and washable markers for each participant.

- **Application:** This visual demonstrates how God erases sin when we're willing to give it up. Attendees should write their sins on index cards with washable markers. Invite attendees forward with their "sin" cards to place them into the water bowl. Continue teaching and give time for sins to be "washed away" by God's forgiveness. Finally, remove the blank cards from the colored water.

- **Contributor:** Jennifer Sakata

I have seen this done with pieces of tile and washable markers. When the speaker poured "living" water over the tiles and pointed out that the words had washed away, the audience gasped with relief.

Image: vecteezy.com

Read the entire chapter that contains this passage. Reflect and pray about its meaning. _____

_____

- What insights are there when considering the historical or situational context? _____

_____

- What speaks to you directly? _____

_____

- How does it apply to your message? _____

_____

- What personal story will you describe to help others apply this truth?_____

_____

- What type of preparation might you need to use the props effectively? _____

_____

15. Scripture: Psalm 139:14

- **Theme:** Comparison

- **Visual Aids:** Use a measuring stick or tape.

- **Application:** Comparison is a deadly game. We tend to compare ourselves to others by our outside traits. Use the measuring tape to measure the length of your arms, the height of your legs, and the size of your foot. Ask if these measurements define who you are as a child of God. Then, highlight this Psalm, reinforcing that God has created each of us unique. He values us by our intrinsic virtues and capabilities.

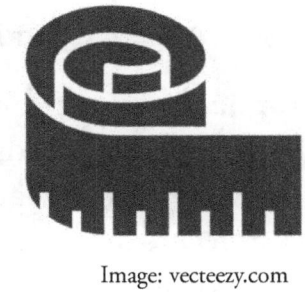

Image: vecteezy.com

Read the entire chapter that contains this passage. Reflect and pray about its meaning. ____

_____

- What insights are there when considering the historical or situational context? _____

_____

- What speaks to you directly? _____

_____

- How does it apply to your message? _____

_____

- What personal story will you describe to help others apply this truth?_____

_____

_____

- What type of preparation might you need to use the props effectively? _____

_____

_____

16. Scripture: Proverbs 3:5-6

- **Theme:** Listen to God's Messages

- **Visual Aids:** Use a microphone, earbuds, and a Bible.

- **Application:** The earbuds represent the messages we listen to in our heads (our own understanding). The microphone represents God's voice reading His Word to re-record over the old messages and acknowledge Him. This can be combined with Philippians 4:8.

Image: vecteezy.com

Read the entire chapter that contains this passage. Reflect and pray about its meaning. _____

_____

- What insights are there when considering the historical or situational context? _____

_____

- What speaks to you directly? _____

_____

- How does it apply to your message? _____

_____

- What personal story will you describe to help others apply this truth?_____

_____

_____

- What type of preparation might you need to use the props effectively? _____

_____

_____

17. Scripture: Proverbs 14:29

Additional Scripture Resource: ***Proverbs 18:7 or James 1:2***

- **Theme:** Uncontrolled Words or Anger

- **Visual Aids:** Use a toothpaste tube and a paper plate.

- **Application:** Explain that the toothpaste represents the words coming from our mouths as you squeeze it onto the paper plate. Invite an audience member to try and put the toothpaste back into the tube. When we do not watch our words, they can come out too fast, and we can't take them back, possibly causing harm and regret.

Read the entire chapter that contains this passage. Reflect and pray about its meaning. _____

_____

- What insights are there when considering the historical or situational context? _____

_____

- What speaks to you directly? _____

_____

- How does it apply to your message? _____

_____

- What personal story will you describe to help others apply this truth?_____

_____

_____

- What type of preparation might you need to use the props effectively? _____

_____

_____

18. Scripture: Proverbs 16:9

Idea One

- **Theme:** God Designs Your Steps.

- **Visual Aid:** Use a map with two different routes highlighted starting from the same spot, diverging, and sometimes intersecting. This works best as a slide projected onto a screen.

- **Application:** We often make plans, thinking we are following God's will. Even when we detour, if we keep our eyes on Him, He knows where we are headed and guides our steps.

Read the entire chapter that contains this passage. Reflect and pray about its meaning. _____

_____

- What insights are there when considering the historical or situational context? _____

_____

- What speaks to you directly? _____

_____

- How does it apply to your message? _____

_____

- What personal story will you describe to help others apply this truth?_____

_____

_____

- What type of preparation might you need to use the props effectively? _____

_____

19. Scripture: Proverbs 16:9  *Idea Two*

- **Theme:** God Designs Your Steps.

- **Visual Aids:** Use a collection of shoes that serve different purposes.

- **Application:** Describe different jobs, activities, and conditions requiring different footwear. Although we may be uncertain about the future, we should trust God's guidance and listen attentively. How can inappropriate footwear indicate disobedience? How do your shoes tell your story? How do your shoes represent where you've been or where God has you now?

Read the entire chapter that contains this passage. Reflect and pray about its meaning. _____

_____

- What insights are there when considering the historical or situational context? _____

_____

- What speaks to you directly? _____

_____

- How does it apply to your message? _____

_____

- What personal story will you describe to help others apply this truth?_____

_____

_____

- What type of preparation might you need to use the props effectively? _____

_____

_____

20. Scripture: Proverbs 26:17–26   Idea One

Additional Scripture Resource: **Ephesians 4:29**

- **Theme:** Gossip

- **Visual Aids:** Use liquid soap to make bubbles.

- **Application:** Dip the wand into the soap and blow out bubbles. Notice how bubbles are created when you blow through the wand. In the same way, your words can create ripples of gossip. One careless remark can spread and cause harm, like bubbles that float far and wide. Remember, your words have power, and it's essential to use them wisely.

Read the entire chapter that contains this passage. Reflect and pray about its meaning. _____

_____

- What insights are there when considering the historical or situational context? _____

_____

- What speaks to you directly? _____

_____

- How does it apply to your message? _____

_____

- What personal story will you describe to help others apply this truth?_____

_____

_____

- What type of preparation might you need to use the props effectively? _____

_____

_____

21. Scripture: Proverbs 26:17–26   Idea Two

Additional Scripture Resource: *Ephesians 4:29*

- **Theme:** Gossip

- **Visual Aids:** Use pencils.

- **Application:** Engage four volunteers and equip each with a pencil. Describe a fictional hurtful situation. Form a half circle open to the audience. Encourage each person to share their actions or words that could have contributed to or perpetuated the issue under discussion. As they do so, guide them to bring their pencils toward the circle's center. This illustrates how their words acted as fuel, intensifying the situation. Reflect on how a fire escalates with more fuel. This activity underscores our collective responsibility to shape the situation.

Now, stress the importance of each participant committing to an action that helps alleviate the situation. As each person expresses a solution, have them pull their pencil out of the circle and point out the dwindling of the imagined flame. Unfueled flames eventually die out.

Read the entire chapter that contains this passage. Reflect and pray about its meaning. _____

_____

- What insights are there when considering the historical or situational context? _____

_____

- What speaks to you directly? _____

_____

- How does it apply to your message? _____

_____

- What personal story will you describe to help others apply this truth?_____

_____

- What type of preparation might you need to use the props effectively? _____

_____

22. Scripture: Proverbs 27:17

- **Theme:** Mentoring

- **Visual Aids:** Use an iron knife sharpener and a dull knife, a piece of fruit, and a cutting board.

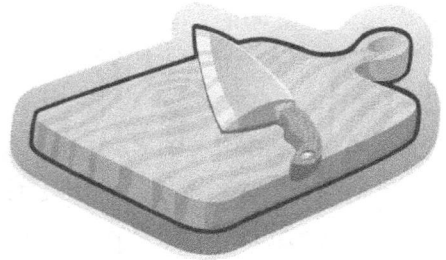

- **Application:** Use the dulled knife to try and cut the fruit. Sharpen the knife with the knife sharpener, then demonstrate how the iron sharpened the knife to strengthen it and improve its performance. Discuss how we are called to walk alongside others, support, teach, and even admonish them to help them step into their purpose.

- **Contributor:** Kris Howsley King

Read the entire chapter that contains this passage. Reflect and pray about its meaning. _____

_____

- What insights are there when considering the historical or situational context? _____

_____

- What speaks to you directly? _____

_____

- How does it apply to your message? _____

_____

- What personal story will you describe to help others apply this truth?_____

_____

_____

- What type of preparation might you need to use the props effectively? _____

_____

_____

23. Scripture: Proverbs 31:10

*Additional Scripture Resource: **1 Samuel 16:7***

- **Theme:** God Sees You as Precious

- **Visual Aids:** Use gemstones: synthetic, cut, and raw.

- **Application:** Display the stones where attendees can pick them up and guess their value.

   In the presentation, discuss each stone. Examples of gems are as follows:

   a. A lab-created gem. Synthetics look real, but the naturally created ones are more valuable.

   b. A natural gem-like emerald or amethyst hardened into a granite host is unusable. (A hardened heart may never reach its full potential.)

   c. An uncut gem, like a ruby or diamond, even a piece of coal. Each gem is only made beautiful through pressure, heat, harsh elements, and cutting. While the gem develops over time, it remains buried, unseen, and inaccessible, but God always knows where the rock is and his plan for its future. God uses harsh things to bring us to our full potential. Through it all, He looks at you and says, "You are precious."

- **Contributor:** Lisa Saruga

Read the entire chapter that contains this passage. Reflect and pray about its meaning. _____

_____

- What insights are there when considering the historical or situational context? _____

_____

- What speaks to you directly? _____

_____

- How does it apply to your message? _____

_____

- What personal story will you describe to help others apply this truth?_____

_____

- What type of preparation might you need to use the props effectively? _____

_____

24. Scripture: Ecclesiastes 4:12

- **Theme:** Strength with Three Strands

- **Visual Aids:** Use four pieces of brightly colored, flimsy string, and one clear piece of fishing line.

- **Application:** Weave two pieces of the string together and tug hard; they stretch and break. Then, braid the clear line with two pieces of the same string and tug. It's much more substantial. The clear line represents the strength God brings when He is woven into a relationship.

Image: vecteezy.com

Read the entire chapter that contains this passage. Reflect and pray about its meaning. _____

_____

- What insights are there when considering the historical or situational context? _____

_____

- What speaks to you directly? _____

_____

- How does it apply to your message? _____

_____

- What personal story will you describe to help others apply this truth?_____

_____

_____

- What type of preparation might you need to use the props effectively? _____

_____

_____

25. Scripture: Isaiah 49:15b–16

- **Theme:** God Never Forgets You

- **Visual Aid:** Use Sharpies. Have a picture of a name written on a hand. This works well on a slide projected on a screen.

- **Application:** Ask this question: "Have you ever written a reminder on your hand?" Write your name on your hand with a Sharpie and encourage the audience to do the same. Look at it and discuss with a partner what it means to them that the God of the universe has their names written on His hand.

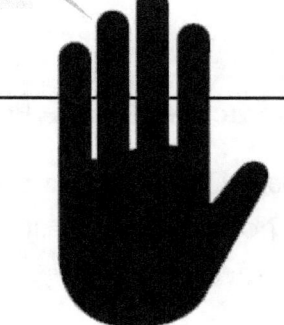

Some translations use the word "written" instead of "carved," "engraved," or "inscribed." If you use this analogy, be sure to use a translation that uses the word "written."

Image: vecteezy.com

Read the entire chapter that contains this passage. Reflect and pray about its meaning. _____

_____

- What insights are there when considering the historical or situational context? _____

_____

- What speaks to you directly? _____

_____

- How does it apply to your message? _____

_____

- What personal story will you describe to help others apply this truth?_____

_____

_____

- What type of preparation might you need to use the props effectively? _____

_____

26. Scripture: Isaiah 64:8

- **Theme:** God is the Potter, and We Are the Clay

- **Visual Aids:** Use a piece of moldable clay and three pieces of pottery in three stages (fired but unpainted, painted, and finished).

- **Application:** Using the clay, you can shape it while speaking, smash it, and reshape it again, much like God does with us. It is an excellent visual describing the refining process. The piece must be baked in a hot kiln between each stage. Representing our difficult trials that feel like walking through fire. The three stages of pottery fired—unpainted, painted, and the finished piece —help to highlight the changes we go through as God continues to form us.

Read the entire chapter that contains this passage. Reflect and pray about its meaning. _____

_____

- What insights are there when considering the historical or situational context? _____

_____

- What speaks to you directly? _____

_____

- How does it apply to your message? _____

_____

- What personal story will you describe to help others apply this truth?_____

_____

_____

- What type of preparation might you need to use the props effectively? _____

_____

_____

27. Scripture: Jeremiah 29:11–13  *Idea One*

- **Theme:** Finding God's Presence and Purpose in Challenging Times

- **Visual Aids:** Use tangled necklaces or Christmas lights.

- **Application:** When life circumstances are compounded by tragedies, personal pain, and loss, it can cause confusion, discouragement, and disillusionment. Much like these tangled necklaces or knotted Christmas lights, our lives can feel like a tangled mess. But we have a God who knows every knot and tangle and has a purpose and a plan to unravel the mess.

- **Contributor:** Amberly Neese

Image: vecteezy.com

Read the entire chapter that contains this passage. Reflect and pray about its meaning. _____

_____

- What insights are there when considering the historical or situational context? _____

_____

- What speaks to you directly? _____

_____

- How does it apply to your message? _____

_____

- What personal story will you describe to help others apply this truth?_____

_____

_____

- What type of preparation might you need to use the props effectively? _____

_____

_____

28. *Scripture: Jeremiah 29:11–13*   *Idea Two*

- **Theme:** God Has Plans for You

- **Visual Aids:** Use a jigsaw puzzle with the box and picture.

- **Application:** Hold up the picture on the box of the jigsaw puzzle. God knows the picture and plans for our life, but we only have pieces. Then, open the box and pour out the pieces. Describe the different ways we try to put puzzles together. Similarly, we can become confused, discouraged, and frustrated with the pieces of our lives we are trying to assemble. Believing and trusting God in these challenging times is our source of strength and comfort.

Image: vecteezy.com

Read the entire chapter that contains this passage. Reflect and pray about its meaning. _____

_____

- What insights are there when considering the historical or situational context? _____

_____

- What speaks to you directly? _____

_____

- How does it apply to your message? _____

_____

- What personal story will you describe to help others apply this truth?_____

_____

_____

- What type of preparation might you need to use the props effectively? _____

_____

_____

29. Scripture: Jeremiah 31:3

- **Theme:** You Are Loved by God.

- **Visual Aid:** Make a thin paper sign to be worn across the chest, hanging from a ribbon or string around the neck. Add large text: IALAC (I Am Lovable and Capable).[12]

- **Application:** Open the discussion by sharing experiences that negatively impacted your self-esteem while ripping pieces off the IALAC sign. Explain that each person wears an invisible IALAC sign, and depending upon the day, they may have already lost bits and pieces of their sign, looking for love and acceptance from outside sources. Finally, tear what's remaining of the sign and say, "The only way I made it was to discover and accept how much God loves me and designed me as His unique creation." This provides an opportunity to offer an invitation to receive Christ.

- **Contributor:** Carol Kent

Read the entire chapter that contains this passage. Reflect and pray about its meaning. _____

_____

- What insights are there when considering the historical or situational context? _____

_____

- What speaks to you directly? _____

_____

- How does it apply to your message? _____

_____

- What personal story will you describe to help others apply this truth?_____

_____

- What type of preparation might you need to use the props effectively? _____

_____

[12] Sidney Simon, *I Am Loveable and Capable: A Modern Allegory on the Classic Put-Down* (Chicago: Argus Communication, 1973).

30. Scripture: Zechariah 4

- **Theme:** Light Your World

- **Visual Aids:** Use one bowl, two branches, a table, and a candle.

- **Application:** The lamp in the temple was filled with oil and was lit daily. When the Spirit comes and fills his people, He will be the never-ending source of oil to keep the light burning. The image in Zechariah 4 is a prophetic vision of those filled with the Holy Spirit sharing the light of Jesus.

- **Contributor:** Carol Tetzlaff

Ask three volunteers to stand shoulder to shoulder. The middle person holds the bowl and lights the candle on the table. The other volunteers hold branches in their outside hands and touch the bowl with their inside hands.

Image: vecteezy.com

Read the entire chapter that contains this passage. Reflect and pray about its meaning. _____

_____

- What insights are there when considering the historical or situational context? _____

_____

- What speaks to you directly? _____

_____

- How does it apply to your message? _____

_____

- What personal story will you describe to help others apply this truth?_____

_____

_____

- What type of preparation might you need to use the props effectively? _____

_____

_____

Bringing Scripture to Life

❧

Visual Aids for New Testament

31. Scripture: Matthew 4:18–21

- **Theme:** Being a Fisher of Men

- **Visual Aids:** Use a fishing pole, bait, a Bible, and a watch or clock.

- **Application:** Passion, knowledge of preferences, and patience are needed to be a successful fisherman. The chart below describes how to use each prop to explain this message.

Attributes	Visual Aids	What you need as a fisherman.	What you need as a fisher of people.
Passion	Pole	Desire to fish.	Desire to witness.
Knowledge of preferences	Bait/Bible	What kind of fish. Knowledge of where they hang out. What equipment to use and type of bait.	Knowledge of what kind of people they are. Knowledge of where they hang out. Knowledge of their areas of interest. Knowledge of their needs.
Patience: avoid expectations	Watch or Clock	Time	Listen to them and meet them where they are emotionally. Let the Holy Spirit be your guide and ask God to be the One who works in their hearts.

Read the entire chapter that contains this passage. Reflect and pray about its meaning. _____

_____

- What insights are there when considering the historical or situational context? _____

_____

- How does it apply to your message? _____

_____

- What personal story will you describe to help others apply this truth?_____

_____

- What type of preparation might you need to use the props effectively? _____

_____

32. Scripture: Matthew 5:14–16

- **Theme:** Being the Light of the World

- **Visual Aid:** Use a solar light that has been charged so that when you cover the solar panel, it lights up.

- **Application:** Hold the solar light and demonstrate how it lights up only when you cover the sensor. However, for this to happen, it must be fully charged by exposure to the sun for a while. Similarly, we can charge and energize our spiritual lives by spending time with the Son (Jesus), enabling us to shine His light in dark places.

- **Contributor:** Milo Miller (with permission)

Image: vecteezy.com

Read the entire chapter that contains this passage. Reflect and pray about its meaning. ____

_____

- What insights are there when considering the historical or situational context? _____

_____

- What speaks to you directly? _____

_____

- How does it apply to your message? _____

_____

- What personal story will you describe to help others apply this truth?_____

_____

_____

- What type of preparation might you need to use the props effectively? _____

_____

33. Scripture: Matthew 5:24

- **Theme:** Mistakes/Healing/Reconciliation

- **Visual Aids:** Gather an assortment of sharpened pencils, some with erasers and some without.

- **Application:** Points on pencils have the potential to make mistakes and/or hurt others. Erasers represent forgiveness, acceptance, and healing in relationships that have been injured. A broken pencil can represent a broken relationship and be taped together to represent healing. Even though the pencil won't heal, use it to describe the healing process of a broken bone. Just like our bodies need time to heal, so do relationships.

Read the entire chapter that contains this passage. Reflect and pray about its meaning. _____

_____

- What insights are there when considering the historical or situational context? _____

_____

- What speaks to you directly? _____

_____

- How does it apply to your message? _____

_____

- What personal story will you describe to help others apply this truth?_____

_____

_____

- What type of preparation might you need to use the props effectively? _____

_____

34. Scripture: Matthew 6:21

*Additional Scripture Resources: **Luke 12:34; Colossians 3:12; Philippians 4:8***

- **Theme:** Where Is Your Treasure?

- **Visual Aids:** Use a treasure box with items symbolizing idols and distractions. Suggestions could include the following, but pick ones you can address: a wallet, a cell phone, a packed planner, a wine bottle, and a black cloth representing grief. Put some large jewels in there too. Candy rings or colored stones also work well.

- **Application:** We allow a variety of activities to consume our focus and energy. Do they bring us closer to God? What should we be valuing? What items might replace those distracting us from God's purposes? As you bring out each item, tell your story and how these items represent where your focus has been detoured. Then, when you bring out the jewels, name the fruits of the spirit, the qualities in Colossians 3:12 or Philippians 4:8, and what changes you made to focus on these. For example, you might share how the cell phone could have notifications removed and replaced with reminders to pray.

———————————————— ❧ ————————————————

Read the entire chapter that contains this passage. Reflect and pray about its meaning. _____

_____

- What insights are there when considering the historical or situational context? _____

_____

- What speaks to you directly? _____

_____

- How does it apply to your message? _____

_____

- What personal story will you describe to help others apply this truth?_____

_____

- What type of preparation might you need to use the props effectively? _____

_____

35. Scripture: Matthew 6:33

Additional Scripture Resource: **Psalm 37:5**

- **Theme:** Seek First—Setting Priorities

- **Visual Aids:** You will need two identical sets of the following:
  - two glass containers, 1-2 quarts in size
  - three or four golf balls
  - two cups of pebbles
  - two cups of sand

- **Application:** The golf balls symbolize your main priorities, and each smaller object represents items of less importance. Demonstrate what not prioritizing looks like, by putting the sand in first, then a few golf balls, then some pebbles, and eventually, the jar fills without room for anything else. With prioritization and planning, everything will fit. Place the largest objects (representing our highest priorities) into the container first. Then, add the pebbles and, finally, the sand. This one requires practice before implementation.[13]

Read the entire chapter that contains this passage. Reflect and pray about its meaning. _____

_____

- What insights are there when considering the historical or situational context? _____

_____

- What speaks to you directly? _____

_____

- How does it apply to your message? _____

_____

- What personal story will you describe to help others apply this truth?_____

_____

- What type of preparation might you need to use the props effectively? _____

_____

[13] Jeremy Wright, "Time Management: The Pickle Jar Theory," A List Apart, June 22, 2002, https://alistapart.com/article/pickle/.

36. Scripture: Matthew 10:31

Image: vecteezy.com

- **Theme:** Value

- **Visual Aid:** Use a fake hundred-dollar bill.

- **Application:** Discuss the value of an actual hundred-dollar bill. Get the fake one dirty, put it in water, and even rip it, then ask if it were an actual hundred-dollar bill, would it lose its value? Many of us feel disqualified or less valued because of our past. But God knows your shameful past and still sees you as valuable.

Read the entire chapter that contains this passage. Reflect and pray about its meaning. _____

_____

- What insights are there when considering the historical or situational context? _____

_____

- What speaks to you directly? _____

_____

- How does it apply to your message? _____

_____

- What personal story will you describe to help others apply this truth?_____

_____

_____

- What type of preparation might you need to use the props effectively? _____

_____

_____

37. Scripture: Matthew 11:28–30, *Idea One*

- **Theme:** It's Not Yours to Carry

- **Visual Aids:** Use a necklace, a scarf, and two garbage bags filled with pillows and tied together. Position the tie around your neck so the bags hang in front. One bag represents disappointment and hurt feelings; the other represents bitterness and unforgiveness.

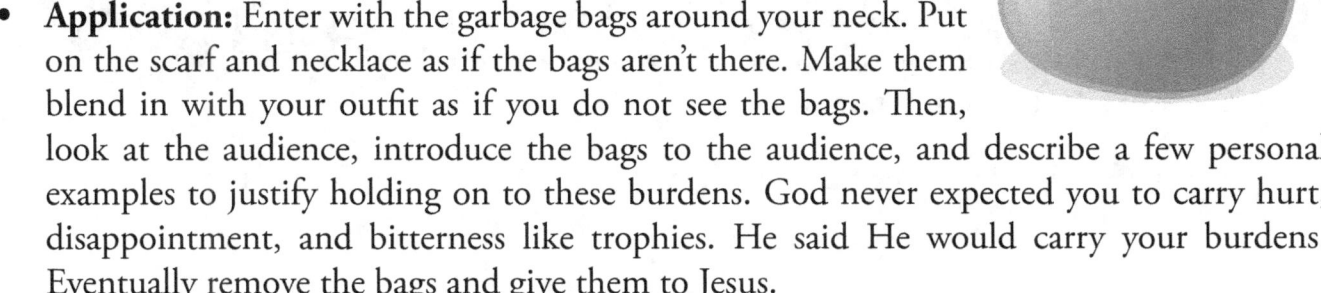

- **Application:** Enter with the garbage bags around your neck. Put on the scarf and necklace as if the bags aren't there. Make them blend in with your outfit as if you do not see the bags. Then, look at the audience, introduce the bags to the audience, and describe a few personal examples to justify holding on to these burdens. God never expected you to carry hurt, disappointment, and bitterness like trophies. He said He would carry your burdens. Eventually remove the bags and give them to Jesus.

- **Contributor:** Jackie Hayden

Read the entire chapter that contains this passage. Reflect and pray about its meaning. _____

_____

- What insights are there when considering the historical or situational context? _____

_____

- What speaks to you directly? _____

_____

- How does it apply to your message? _____

_____

- What personal story will you describe to help others apply this truth?_____

_____

- What type of preparation might you need to use the props effectively? _____

_____

38. Scripture: Matthew 11:28-30  *Idea Two*

- **Theme:** Don't Carry Your Burdens by Yourself

- **Visual Aids:** Use a backpack filled with rocks or symbols representing specific worries (a family picture, car keys, cooking pan, Bible, child-sized clothing, an alcohol bottle, a wallet, checkbook, and/or prescriptions).

- **Application:** Take out each item and name the worry and concern. Then, symbolically, give it to God. Ask a volunteer to help you hold the backpack to represent the support of a loving community.

Read the entire chapter that contains this passage. Reflect and pray about its meaning. _____

_____

- What insights are there when considering the historical or situational context? _____

_____

- What speaks to you directly? _____

_____

- How does it apply to your message? _____

_____

- What personal story will you describe to help others apply this truth?_____

_____

_____

- What type of preparation might you need to use the props effectively? _____

_____

_____

39. Scripture: Matthew 28:19

- **Theme:** Trinity (Three Ideas)

- **Visual Aids:**
    a. Hard-boiled egg (shell, yolk, white)
    b. Water, steam, ice
    c. Any fruit (skin, pulp, seeds)

- **Application:** In our finite human mind, it's hard to understand three in one. These items help demonstrate how one object can identify three things, helping to symbolize the image of the Trinity of Father, Son, and Holy Ghost into one being. However, the Trinity is three unique beings in one and is far more powerful than these symbols.

Read the entire chapter that contains this passage. Reflect and pray about its meaning. ____

_____

- What insights are there when considering the historical or situational context? _____

_____

- What speaks to you directly? _____

_____

- How does it apply to your message? _____

_____

- What personal story will you describe to help others apply this truth?_____

_____

_____

- What type of preparation might you need to use the props effectively? _____

_____

_____

40. Scripture: Mark 2:27–28

Additional Scripture Resource: **Galatians 1:10**

- **Theme:** Making Time for the Sabbath

- **Visual Aids:** Use two pieces of paper with identical text written on both. One should have no margins or punctuation, while the second example is written with the correct punctuation. This is best displayed on a slide projected on a screen.

- **Application:** We tend to schedule ourselves so tightly that we don't have time to breathe. Compare the exact text with margins to the one without margins. The one with punctuation and margins is easier to read but consumes more area. However, the spaces for margins and punctuation represent time and opportunities for rest, rejuvenation, and quiet time with the Lord for prayer, praise, Scripture reading, and listening to Him. The spaces also allow time for the Sabbath and solitude.

Wetendtoscheduleourselvessotightlythatwedon'thavetimetobreathe. Comparetheexacttextwithmarginstotheonewithoutmargins. Theonewithpunctuationandmarginsiseasiertoreadbutconsumesmorearea. However,thespacesformarginsandpunctuationrepresenttimeandopportunitiesforrestrejuvenation,andquiettimewiththeLordforprayer,praise,Scripturereading,andlisteningtoHim. ThespacesalsoallowtimefortheSabbathandsolitude.

Read the entire chapter that contains this passage. Reflect and pray about its meaning. _____

_____

- What insights are there when considering the historical or situational context? _____

_____

- What speaks to you directly? _____

_____

- How does it apply to your message? _____

_____

- What personal story will you describe to help others apply this truth?_____

_____

- What type of preparation might you need to use the props effectively? _____

_____

41. Scripture: Luke 6:46–49

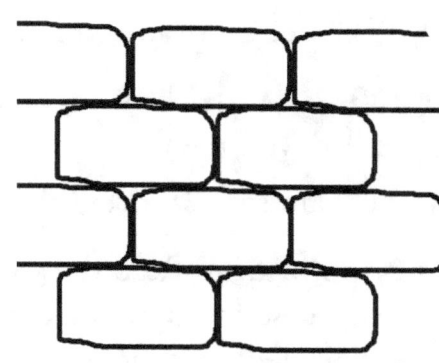

- **Theme:** Building Your House, Your Faith, on the Rock

- **Visual Aids:** Use a small box with sand, a piece of slate or tile, two houses made from toy blocks, a Bible, some modern-interest magazines, and a cell phone.

- **Application:** Jesus explains how faith built on Him, the Rock, will withstand storms. You shake the house on the sand, and it will collapse. You shake the house on the slate, and it stays standing. How do we nurture our spirit? Do we spend all our downtime seeking wisdom from social media and magazines? These are like the sand and will not support us during storms. However, the slate or tile represents the foundation established by spending time in the Word of God and nurturing our relationship with Christ. He will give us support and strength to survive the most devastating storms.

Read the entire chapter that contains this passage. Reflect and pray about its meaning. _____

_____

- What insights are there when considering the historical or situational context? _____

_____

- What speaks to you directly? _____

_____

- How does it apply to your message? _____

_____

- What personal story will you describe to help others apply this truth?_____

_____

_____

- What type of preparation might you need to use the props effectively? _____

_____

42. Scripture: Luke 8:4–15

*Additional Scripture Resource: **Matthew 13:3–9; Mark 4:1–9***

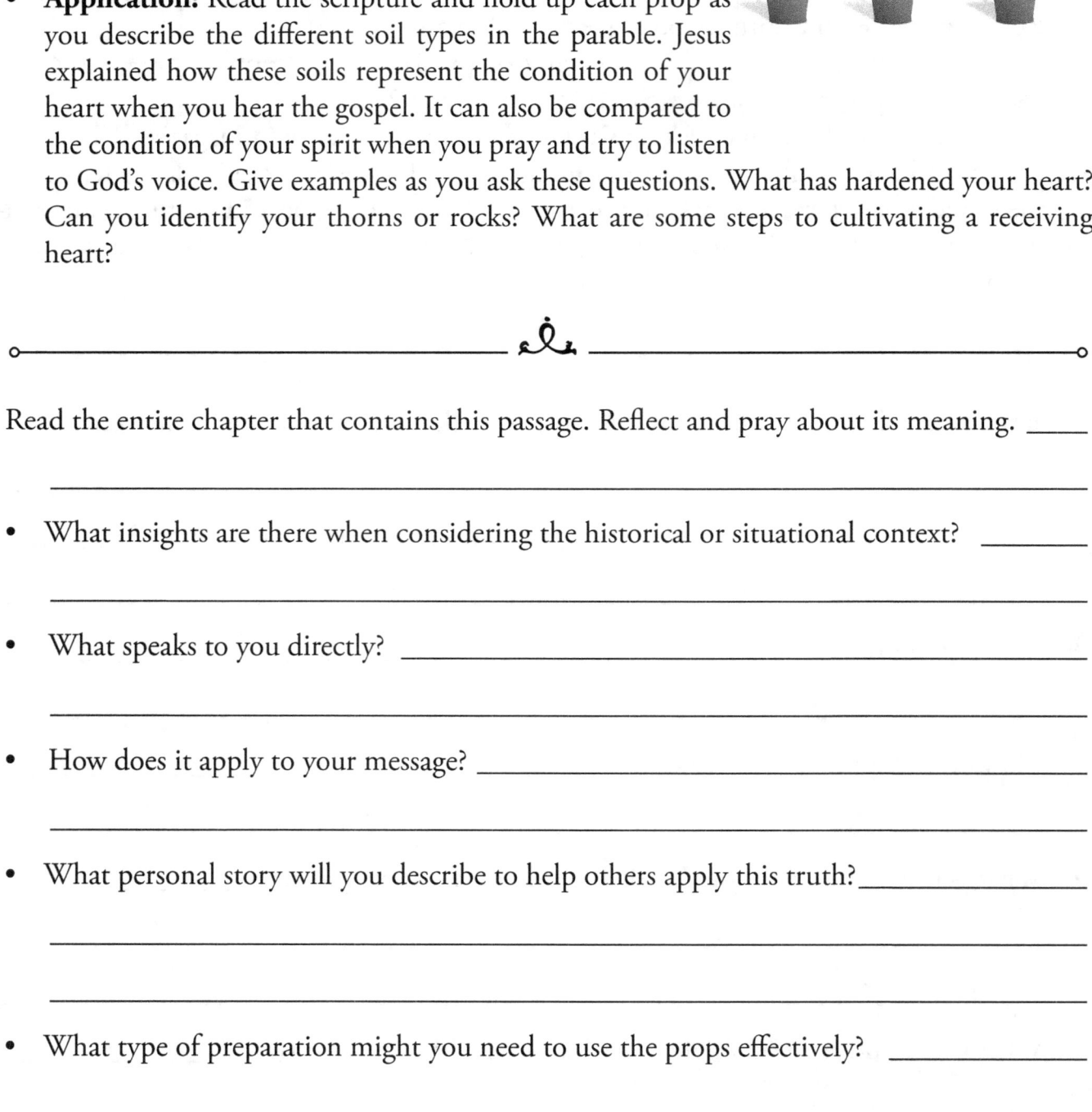

- **Theme:** Cultivating a Receiving Heart

- **Visual Aids:** Use seeds or seed packets and four flowerpots filled with the following:

  1) hard soil, 2) rocks, 3) thorns, and 4) a healthy plant.

- **Application:** Read the scripture and hold up each prop as you describe the different soil types in the parable. Jesus explained how these soils represent the condition of your heart when you hear the gospel. It can also be compared to the condition of your spirit when you pray and try to listen to God's voice. Give examples as you ask these questions. What has hardened your heart? Can you identify your thorns or rocks? What are some steps to cultivating a receiving heart?

Read the entire chapter that contains this passage. Reflect and pray about its meaning. _____

_____

- What insights are there when considering the historical or situational context? _____

_____

- What speaks to you directly? _____

_____

- How does it apply to your message? _____

_____

- What personal story will you describe to help others apply this truth?_____

_____

_____

- What type of preparation might you need to use the props effectively? _____

_____

43. Scripture: Luke 10:27

*Additional Scripture Resources; **Matthew 22:37; Mark 12:30***

- **Theme:** Loving God with Heart, Mind, Soul, and Strength

- **Visual Aids:** Use a heart-shaped picture, paper, or object, hat, shawl, and an exercise weight.

- **Application:** Hold up each object as you describe how loving God with each of the four areas differs: heart: loving with our emotions (heart object), head: loving with our thoughts (hat), soul: loving with our awareness (shawl), and strength: loving with our actions (weight).

Read the entire chapter that contains this passage. Reflect and pray about its meaning. _____

_____

- What insights are there when considering the historical or situational context? _____

_____

- What speaks to you directly? _____

_____

- How does it apply to your message? _____

_____

- What personal story will you describe to help others apply this truth?_____

_____

_____

- What type of preparation might you need to use the props effectively? _____

_____

44. Scripture: Luke 12:34

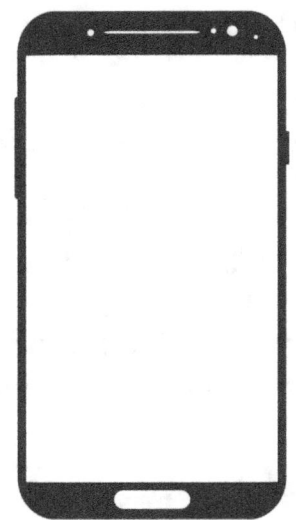

- **Theme:** Establishing Christ-Centered Priorities

- **Visual Aids:** Use a smartphone and/or a planner and a checkbook.

- **Application:** Priorities are evident in the way we spend our time and money. What does our current use of time and money reveal about our priorities? How could we adjust our current expenditures to make room for our precious resources to be used to glorify God?

- **Contributor:** Angie Baughman

Read the entire chapter that contains this passage. Reflect and pray about its meaning. _____

_____

- What insights are there when considering the historical or situational context? _____

_____

- What speaks to you directly? _____

- How does it apply to your message? _____

_____

- What personal story will you describe to help others apply this truth?_____

_____

_____

- What type of preparation might you need to use the props effectively? _____

_____

_____

45. Scripture: Luke 22:14–20

Additional Scripture Resource: **Matthew 26:26–30; Mark 14:22–26; 1 Corinthians 11:23–25**

- **Theme:** Last Supper/Communion

- **Visual Aids:** Use a loaf of bread and a wine goblet.

- **Application:** Have these items on an altar or a table in front of you so you can lift them up as you describe Christ's actions during the Last Supper, much like a pastor would do when introducing Communion.

Read the entire chapter that contains this passage. Reflect and pray about its meaning. _____

_____

- What insights are there when considering the historical or situational context? _____

_____

- What speaks to you directly? _____

_____

- How does it apply to your message? _____

_____

- What personal story will you describe to help others apply this truth?_____

_____

_____

- What type of preparation might you need to use the props effectively? _____

_____

_____

46. Scripture: John 3:16

Idea One

- **Theme:** God's Gift of Eternal Life

- **Visual Aid:** Use a beautifully wrapped present that can be opened easily during the presentation.

- **Application:** Compare the difference between head knowledge about Jesus and heart knowledge of a relationship with Jesus. Receiving a gift but carrying it around unopened represents head knowledge. However we demonstrate trust and acceptance when we open the gift we have received. This provides an opportunity to extend an invitation to receive Christ.

Image: vecteezy.com

- **Contributor:** Linda Hammond

Read the entire chapter that contains this passage. Reflect and pray about its meaning. _____

_____

- What insights are there when considering the historical or situational context? _____

_____

- What speaks to you directly? _____

_____

- How does it apply to your message? _____

_____

- What personal story will you describe to help others apply this truth?_____

_____

_____

- What type of preparation might you need to use the props effectively? _____

_____

_____

47. Scripture: John 3:16

- **Theme:** Jesus Is the Key

- **Visual Aid:** Use a large brass key.

- **Application:** Knowing Jesus is Lord is the key to eternal life. Thus, we are responsible for sharing this gospel knowledge with others. It is the key that will open the door to new life for others.

- **Contributor:** Kris Howsley King

Read the entire chapter that contains this passage. Reflect and pray about its meaning. _____

_____

- What insights are there when considering the historical or situational context? _____

_____

- What speaks to you directly? _____

_____

- How does it apply to your message? _____

_____

- What personal story will you describe to help others apply this truth?_____

_____

_____

- What type of preparation might you need to use the props effectively? _____

_____

48. Scripture: John 4:14

- **Theme:** Being a Flow-Through Vessel

- **Visual Aids:** Use a beverage cup with a straw. Other visual aid ideas for this theme include a pipe as a water conduit or a wire conduit for electricity.

- **Application:** We were never created to be the water of life to anyone. The water is the Word, and Jesus is the Word. God designed us like straws. We get to be submerged in Him and then let others drink of Him through our lives. If you find yourself saying things like "They sucked me dry" or "I'm out of gas," it's time to submerge into Christ again because He NEVER runs dry!

- **Contributor:** Marnie Swedberg[14]

Read the entire chapter that contains this passage. Reflect and pray about its meaning. _____

_____

- What insights are there when considering the historical or situational context? _____

_____

- What speaks to you directly? _____

- How does it apply to your message? _____

_____

- What personal story will you describe to help others apply this truth?_____

_____

- What type of preparation might you need to use the props effectively? _____

_____

[14] Marnie Swedberg, *Flow Through Vessel: How to Master the Habit of Letting God Flow Through You* (Henderson, NV: Gifts of Encouragement, 2015).

49. Scripture: John 4:4-26

- **Theme:** Lessons from the Well

- **Visual Aids:** Use a water pitcher, four glasses, and a bowl to catch the overflow.

- **Application:** As you review this story, pour water from the pitcher into a glass.

  - **Receive a Drink** – The woman came with an empty, thirsting soul (the empty cup), and Jesus filled it to overflow (from the pitcher). The overflow symbolizes sharing the gospel with others. The actual image of the water allows your audience to drink in the message.
  - **Rend a Drink** – Jesus was modeling giving a drink to someone else. Take the full glass and pour it into an empty glass.
  - **Refresh and Restore** – Jesus often drew himself away to a well to restore his weary soul by spending time with the Father. Take an empty glass and fill it from the pitcher, emphasizing the importance of our spiritual replenishment.

Read the entire chapter that contains this passage. Reflect and pray about its meaning. _____

_____

- What insights are there when considering the historical or situational context? _____

_____

- What speaks to you directly? _____

_____

- How does it apply to your message? _____

_____

- What personal story will you describe to help others apply this truth? _____

_____

- What type of preparation might you need to use the props effectively? _____

_____

50. *Scripture: John 6:9–13*

Idea One

- **Theme:** Feeding of the Five Thousand: God Can Use YOU!

- **Visual Aids:** Use blank adhesive name tags for each attendee. At the event's start, ask participants to put on a name tag but leave it blank.

Image: vecteezy.com

- **Application:** We often associate specific skills—enough Bible knowledge, enough resources, or a celebrity name— with success. Name recognition is coveted, but God can use anyone to influence others. The boy who gave his fish and loaves was an influential character though we don't even know his name. Take off your name tag and write on it, "God can use ME!"

- **Contributor:** Kim Cusimano

Read the entire chapter that contains this passage. Reflect and pray about its meaning. _____

_____

- What insights are there when considering the historical or situational context? _____

_____

- What speaks to you directly? _____

_____

- How does it apply to your message? _____

_____

- What personal story will you describe to help others apply this truth?_____

_____

_____

- What type of preparation might you need to use the props effectively? _____

_____

51. Scripture: John 6:9-13

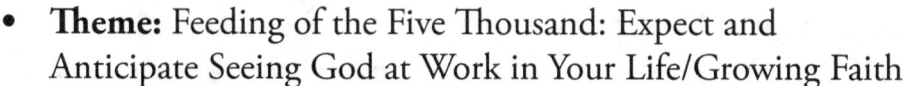

- **Theme:** Feeding of the Five Thousand: Expect and Anticipate Seeing God at Work in Your Life/Growing Faith

- **Visual Aids:** Use a large, empty basket on stage as a visual and/ or an empty basket on each table as part of the centerpiece.

- **Application:** What are you praying for God to do? What are your needs? Ask, "Am I expecting God to help me?" The disciples were not expecting Jesus to feed the people. Surely, filling those baskets with leftovers grew their faith. They started with empty baskets and ended with full ones. What are your empty baskets? What are your needs? Is your faith limited like the disciples', or is it one of anticipation and provision?

- **Contributor:** Kim Cusimano

Read the entire chapter that contains this passage. Reflect and pray about its meaning. _____

_____

- What insights are there when considering the historical or situational context? _____

_____

- What speaks to you directly? _____

_____

- How does it apply to your message? _____

_____

- What personal story will you describe to help others apply this truth? _____

_____

_____

- What type of preparation might you need to use the props effectively? _____

_____

52. Scripture: John 17:3

- **Theme:** Priority of a Relationship with Christ

- **Visual Aids:** Use ten three-by-three-inch blocks.

- **Application:** Build the blocks into a pyramid. I've provided examples for the blocks, but it's important that you assign them to areas that align with your priorities.

  a. Four blocks: On the bottom level are the most basic life needs, such as Jesus, safety, food, and shelter. Feel free to add your own. Make sure a relationship with Christ is on one of the ends of the row.

  b. Three blocks on the second level: friendship, family, and church.

  c. Two blocks on the third level: study and growth.

  d. One block on the top level: a fulfilled life and eternal life; the top level needs to represent your goal.

  Talk about priorities and what would happen if you removed the most important end block, Jesus. The pyramid would crumble. We can't do anything without Christ. He is the Rock of our foundation.

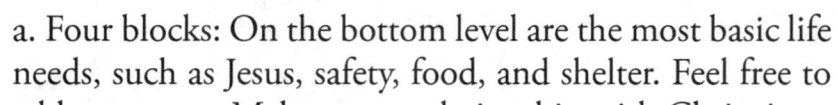

Read the entire chapter that contains this passage. Reflect and pray about its meaning. _____

_____

- What insights are there when considering the historical or situational context? _____

_____

- What speaks to you directly? _____

_____

- How does it apply to your message? _____

_____

- What personal story will you describe to help others apply this truth?_____

_____

- What type of preparation might you need to use the props effectively? _____

_____

53. Scripture: Acts 2:42–47

Additional Scripture Resource: **Galatians 5:22–23**

- **Theme:** Spiritual Formation/Fruits of the Spirit

- **Visual Aid:** Use a fruit tree without any fruit with only a label telling you what kind of fruit tree it is.

- **Application:** Explain that this tree will not produce fruit unless cared for properly. Each fruit tree needs a specific kind of nutrient-rich soil, oxygen, sunlight, and water to produce its fruit. Likewise, we cannot just claim the label of being a Christian. We need to study the Scriptures, participate in a Christian community, apply biblical practices, and serve others to produce the ripe fruit of the Holy Spirit.

- **Contributor:** Aaron Stern

Read the entire chapter that contains this passage. Reflect and pray about its meaning. _____

_____

- What insights are there when considering the historical or situational context? _____

_____

- What speaks to you directly? _____

_____

- How does it apply to your message? _____

_____

- What personal story will you describe to help others apply this truth?_____

_____

_____

- What type of preparation might you need to use the props effectively? _____

_____

54. Scripture: Romans 8:28

- **Theme:** All Things Work Together for Good

- **Visual Aids:** Use the ingredients to make a cake or cookies.

- **Application:** Describe each ingredient and ask the question, "Does it taste good by itself?" Sometimes, we go through experiences and don't understand, but God is combining them all together for our growth. The process takes time, trust, patience. Not being patient is like baking cookies at too high a temperature to get them done sooner. If we skip steps, the result will not be the same as it would have been if we'd followed the directions.

Image: vecteezy.com

Read the entire chapter that contains this passage. Reflect and pray about its meaning. _____

_____

- What insights are there when considering the historical or situational context? _____

_____

- What speaks to you directly? _____

_____

- How does it apply to your message? _____

_____

- What personal story will you describe to help others apply this truth?_____

_____

_____

- What type of preparation might you need to use the props effectively? _____

_____

_____

55. Scripture: Romans 8:35–39

- **Theme:** Breaking Down Walls: Demolishing Walls that Stand in the Way of Healing and Closeness with God

- **Visual Aids:** Use a sledgehammer and stacked bricks or pieces of two-by-fours.

- **Application:** The stacked bricks symbolize the walls built up to hide or forget a time of abuse and violation. If we keep these walls up, they don't allow us to heal. The sledgehammer symbolizes God's ability and our willingness to break down the obstacles and move toward healing. Holding and swinging the sledgehammer represent the energy and emotion it takes to tear down the walls that stand in the way of justice, forgiveness, healing, and a close relationship with God.

- **Contributor:** Lisa Saruga

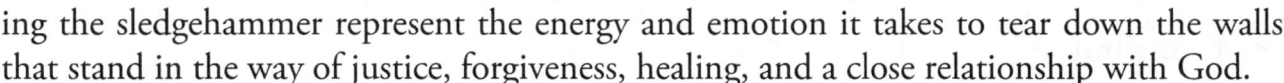

Read the entire chapter that contains this passage. Reflect and pray about its meaning. _____

_____

- What insights are there when considering the historical or situational context? _____

_____

- What speaks to you directly? _____

_____

- How does it apply to your message? _____

_____

- What personal story will you describe to help others apply this truth?_____

_____

_____

- What type of preparation might you need to use the props effectively? _____

_____

56. Scripture: Romans 8:38–39

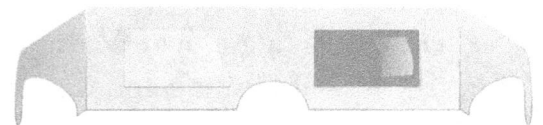

- **Theme:** God's Faithfulness During Trials

- **Visual Aid:** Use 3D glasses.

- **Application:** 3D glasses give the audience a three-dimensional view of different creatures on a movie screen. When the real monsters of life attack, more than a pair of glasses is needed to focus and survive the trials. Challenges in life can bring <u>disappointment</u>, <u>discouragement</u>, and/or <u>desperation</u> (3-Ds of trials). We do not need to handle them alone but depend on the help of the 3D Creator of the universe—the Father, Son, and Holy Spirit. God uses our challenges to help <u>define</u> our identity, <u>discover</u> our purpose, and <u>develop</u> our discipleship (3-Ds of victory).

- **Contributor:** Linda Hammond

Read the entire chapter that contains this passage. Reflect and pray about its meaning. _____

_____

- What insights are there when considering the historical or situational context? _____

_____

- What speaks to you directly? _____

_____

- How does it apply to your message? _____

_____

- What personal story will you describe to help others apply this truth? _____

_____

_____

- What type of preparation might you need to use the props effectively? _____

_____

_____

57. Scripture: 1 Corinthians 12:12–31

*Additional Scripture Resource: **Romans 12:4–13***

- **Theme:** The Body of Christ

- **Visual Aids:** Choose one of the following: puzzle pieces, pieces of a quilt, a large bouquet of different plants and flowers, a large drawing of a person, or ingredients for any recipe (cookies, cake, etc.).

- **Application:** Each of these props is an example of a big picture made from many different parts. No matter your choice of visual aid, it is essential to emphasize the uniqueness of the design and purpose of each piece. Highlight the need for each person's unique gifts and abilities. Explain how they fit together, the beauty in their unity, and the impact on the outcome if one were absent or omitted.

Read the entire chapter that contains this passage. Reflect and pray about its meaning. _____

_____

- What insights are there when considering the historical or situational context? _____

_____

- What speaks to you directly? _____

_____

- How does it apply to your message? _____

_____

- What personal story will you describe to help others apply this truth?_____

_____

_____

- What type of preparation might you need to use the props effectively? _____

_____

_____

58. Scripture: 1 Corinthians 13:1–2, 12

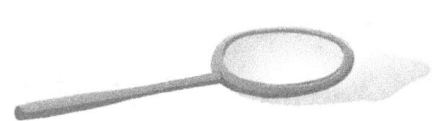

- **Theme:** Love

- **Visual Aids:** Use a mirror, foil, textbooks, and two pan lids.

- **Application:** These props help to highlight the examples Paul uses in this scripture. Textbooks representing knowledge and clanging pan lids are used to emphasize verses 1 and 2. The mirror and foil help to emphasize verse 12.

Read the entire chapter that contains this passage. Reflect and pray about its meaning. _____

_____

- What insights are there when considering the historical or situational context? _____

_____

- What speaks to you directly? _____

_____

- How does it apply to your message? _____

_____

- What personal story will you describe to help others apply this truth?_____

_____

_____

- What type of preparation might you need to use the props effectively? _____

_____

_____

59. Scripture: 1 Corinthians 13:7

- **Theme:** Love Lifts Others

- **Visual Aids:** Use helium balloons.

- **Application:** Just as helium lifts a balloon when released, true agape love does the same for people. "That's what love does—it pursues blindly, unflinchingly, and without end."[15] "I've got some helium balloons to blow up! Love lifts us up—so we can lift each other up."[16]

- **Contributor:** Bob Goff, *Love Does* (used with permission)

Read the entire chapter that contains this passage. Reflect and pray about its meaning. _____

_____

- What insights are there when considering the historical or situational context? _____

_____

- What speaks to you directly? _____

_____

- How does it apply to your message? _____

_____

- What personal story will you describe to help others apply this truth?_____

_____

- What type of preparation might you need to use the props effectively? _____

_____

[15] Bob Goff, *Love Does: Discover a Secretly Incredible Life in an Ordinary World* (Nashville: Thomas Nelson Inc, 2012), 52.

[16] Bob Goff, "I've got some helium balloons," Facebook, December 31, 2013, https://www.facebook.com/bobgoffis/photos/ive-got-some-helium-balloons-to-blow-up-love-lifts-us-up-so-we-can-lift-each-oth/574533145955296/.

60. *Scripture: 1 Corinthians 13:12*

- **Theme:** Not Seeing Things Clearly but Knowing God Has a Greater Purpose.

- **Visual Aids:** Use a rolled-up piece of paper to make a tube. It is impactful to ask the audience to participate in this exercise. You can use a picture with only a portion of it magnified on a slide, but it does not have the same effect.

  I have also used this exercise to symbolize how depression can narrow one's view. Regardless of the age group, it has been a profound activity that promotes a deeper understanding of the situation.

  Image Designed by Brgfx / Freepik

- **Application:** Invite the audience to roll a piece of paper and look around the room. How much can they see? How much are they missing? That's how life is now, but one day, we will see the whole picture. Redirect the attention to the slide and ask the audience if they can identify the picture from the portion that is in focus. That is how life is now, but we will see the whole picture when we fully know. Using the picture in your slide, have the audience guess what it is.

Read the entire chapter that contains this passage. Reflect and pray about its meaning. _____

_____

- What insights are there when considering the historical or situational context? _____

_____

- What speaks to you directly? _____

_____

- How does it apply to your message? _____

_____

- What personal story will you describe to help others apply this truth?_____

_____

- What type of preparation might you need to use the props effectively? _____

_____

69. Scripture: 2 Corinthians 4:7-10

*Additional Scripture Resource: **Psalm 34:18***

- **Theme:** Beauty Amid Brokenness

- **Visual Aids:** Use a pile of broken pieces from a terra cotta pot. Make sure they fit together easily but with a few pieces missing. You also need a glue gun and a battery-operated candle.

- **Application:** We live in a throwaway culture. But God doesn't. While speaking about the treasure of Jesus and the gift of this life, begin piecing the pot back together with quick-dry glue. Dim the lights and insert a battery-operated candle. Note the light as it shines through the cracks.[17]

- **Contributor:** Jennifer Sakata

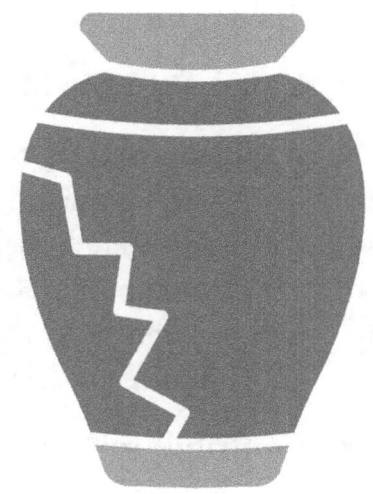

Image: vecteezy.com

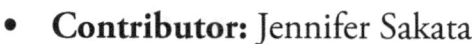

Read the entire chapter that contains this passage. Reflect and pray about its meaning. _____

_____

- What insights are there when considering the historical or situational context? _____

_____

- What speaks to you directly? _____

_____

- How does it apply to your message? _____

_____

- What personal story will you describe to help others apply this truth?_____

_____

_____

- What type of preparation might you need to use the props effectively? _____

_____

[17] Patsy Clairmont, *God Uses Cracked Pots* (Carol Stream, IL: Focus on the Family, 1991).

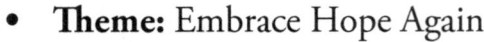

62. *Scripture: 2 Corinthians 4:9*

- **Theme:** Embrace Hope Again

- **Visual Aids:** Use Rock 'Em Sock 'Em Robots.

- **Application:** Use the Rock 'Em Sock 'Em Robots to demonstrate the one-two punch. Give an example of when you were knocked down, and the enemy appeared to win that battle. Remind the audience that he does not win the war. Jesus is always with us, picks us up, and we get up again and keep going.

- **Contributor:** Amy Robnik Joob

Read the entire chapter that contains this passage. Reflect and pray about its meaning. _____

_____

- What insights are there when considering the historical or situational context? _____

_____

- What speaks to you directly? _____

_____

- How does it apply to your message? _____

_____

- What personal story will you describe to help others apply this truth?_____

_____

_____

- What type of preparation might you need to use the props effectively? _____

_____

63. Scripture: Galatians 6:2

- **Theme:** Community Sisterhood: Bearing One Another's Burdens

- **Visual Aids:** Use one rotted two-by-four about three to five feet long and two strong new two-by-fours the same size.

- **Application:** Picture a building frame with old beams that are weak and in dire need of strength. Correcting a problem beam is an easy repair and is usually accomplished by fastening a new beam next to a damaged one and doubling the thickness of the worn-out beam. This is referred to as sistering. In some cases, more support is required, and sister beams must be installed on both sides of the weak beam for even more strength. The sister beams are strengthening the weakened beam, and all three are now "bearing" the weight together.

- **Contributor:** Marie Beck

———————————————————— ❧ ————————————————————

Read the entire chapter that contains this passage. Reflect and pray about its meaning. _____

_____

- What insights are there when considering the historical or situational context? _____

_____

- What speaks to you directly? _____

_____

- How does it apply to your message? _____

_____

- What personal story will you describe to help others apply this truth?_____

_____

- What type of preparation might you need to use the props effectively? _____

_____

64. *Scripture: Galatians 6:2*  *Idea Two*

- **Theme:** Stress

- **Visual Aid:** Use a large ball of yarn.

- **Application:** Toss the ball into the audience and have the one who catches it shout out a stressful situation. Invite them to hold onto the yarn before tossing the ball to another person. Repeat this process with each person until you have a web of yarn between you, representing confusion and stress. Have them pull it tight to represent stressing others. Yet, when they draw closer, the stress lessens, symbolizing strength in the body of Christ.

Read the entire chapter that contains this passage. Reflect and pray about its meaning. _____

_____

- What insights are there when considering the historical or situational context? _____

_____

- What speaks to you directly? _____

_____

- How does it apply to your message? _____

_____

- What personal story will you describe to help others apply this truth?_____

_____

_____

- What type of preparation might you need to use the props effectively? _____

_____

_____

65. Scripture: Galatians 6:4

- **Theme:** Do What God Created You to Do

- **Visual Aids:** Use an old blender and an old toaster. Bread and smoothie ingredients can be used as props or added to the appliances to bring the example to life. Bring ingredients in sealed containers, extension cords, and towels if you plan to put the smoothie ingredients into the toaster (if you do, make sure the toaster is not plugged in.) Putting a piece of bread into the blender is less messy.

- **Application:** The blender does not compete with the toaster. It never measures itself against what the toaster can do because it was created to blend. We are unique and created on purpose, for a purpose. Measuring ourselves against others removes us from who our Creator intended us to be.

- **Contributor:** Nicole Langman

Read the entire chapter that contains this passage. Reflect and pray about its meaning. _____

_____

- What insights are there when considering the historical or situational context? _____

_____

- What speaks to you directly? _____

_____

- How does it apply to your message? _____

_____

- What personal story will you describe to help others apply this truth?_____

_____

- What type of preparation might you need to use the props effectively? _____

_____

66. *Scripture: Ephesians 1:7*

or any verse on forgiveness

- **Theme:** Forgiveness

- **Visual Aids:** Use a glass punch bowl or clear pitcher, food coloring, a spoon, and a pitcher with bleach and water.

- **Application:** The bowl filled with water symbolizes our life. As you tell your story, drop food coloring into the water, representing failures and challenges, and stir until the water is murky. The pitcher with bleach in it represents Jesus. His forgiveness and redemption have the power to wash our sins away. Pour this bleach mixture into the colored water and stir. Practice this so you have the right amounts to make the bleach clear the food coloring.

- **Contributor:** The Reverend Donald Merrill, 1920–2013 (my father)

Read the entire chapter that contains this passage. Reflect and pray about its meaning. _____

_____

- What insights are there when considering the historical or situational context? _____

_____

- What speaks to you directly? _____

_____

- How does it apply to your message? _____

_____

- What personal story will you describe to help others apply this truth? _____

_____

_____

- What type of preparation might you need to use the props effectively? _____

_____

67. Scripture: Ephesians 2:10

- **Theme:** We Are His Masterpiece

- **Visual Aids:** Use unique cups, plates, vases, and serving dishes.

- **Application:** God, the master designer, creates us for distinct purposes. Describe the distinctive beauty and various uses of the displayed dishes.

Read the entire chapter that contains this passage. Reflect and pray about its meaning. _____

_____

- What insights are there when considering the historical or situational context? _____

_____

- What speaks to you directly? _____

_____

- How does it apply to your message? _____

_____

- What personal story will you describe to help others apply this truth?_____

_____

_____

- What type of preparation might you need to use the props effectively? _____

_____

_____

68. Scripture: Ephesians 4:26-27   *Idea One*

- **Theme:** Controlling Anger

- **Visual Aids:** Use a balloon, a marker, and a pin.

- **Application:** As your message describes the events that added to your anger, write them on the balloon. Then, pop it when it is covered with words. Next, blow up a second balloon. Write the same things on this balloon, but let the air out slowly, symbolizing the importance of discussing the issue, not harboring it. Do not go to bed angry.

Read the entire chapter that contains this passage. Reflect and pray about its meaning. ____

_____

- What insights are there when considering the historical or situational context? _____

_____

- What speaks to you directly? _____

_____

- How does it apply to your message? _____

_____

- What personal story will you describe to help others apply this truth?_____

_____

_____

- What type of preparation might you need to use the props effectively? _____

_____

_____

69. Scripture: Ephesians 4:26–27 — Idea Two

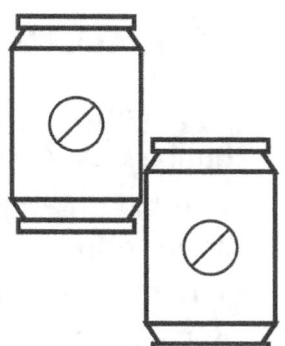

- **Theme:** Controlling Anger

- **Visual Aids:** Use two unopened soda cans or bottles and towels.

- **Application:** As your message describes the events that added to your anger, shake both soda cans or bottles. Then, ask the audience what would happen if you opened them immediately. Let one sit for a while, symbolizing the need to wait before we respond angrily. Open the other one slowly, letting air out gradually, symbolizing the importance of discussing the issue, not harboring it. Do not go to bed angry.

- **Contributor:** Marnie Swedberg

Read the entire chapter that contains this passage. Reflect and pray about its meaning. _____

_____

- What insights are there when considering the historical or situational context? _____

_____

- What speaks to you directly? _____

_____

- How does it apply to your message? _____

_____

- What personal story will you describe to help others apply this truth?_____

_____

_____

- What type of preparation might you need to use the props effectively? _____

_____

70. Scripture: Ephesians 4:29

Idea One

Additional Scripture Resource: ***Proverbs 26:17–26***

- **Theme:** Gossip

- **Visual Aid:** Use liquid soap to make bubbles.

- **Application:** Dip the wand into the soap and blow out bubbles. Notice how bubbles are created when you blow through the wand. In the same way, your words can create ripples of gossip. One careless remark can spread and cause harm, like bubbles that float far and wide. Remember, your words have power, and using them wisely is essential.

Read the entire chapter that contains this passage. Reflect and pray about its meaning. _____

_____

- What insights are there when considering the historical or situational context? _____

_____

- What speaks to you directly? _____

_____

- How does it apply to your message? _____

_____

- What personal story will you describe to help others apply this truth?_____

_____

_____

- What type of preparation might you need to use the props effectively? _____

_____

_____

71. Scripture: Ephesians 4:29

Idea Two

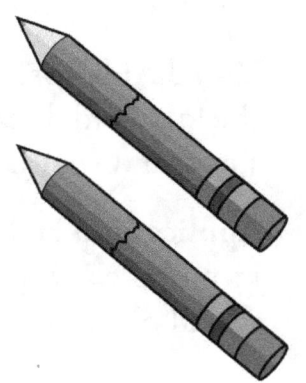

- **Theme:** Gossip

- **Visual Aids:** Use pencils.

- **Application:** Each person who shares a rumor or gossip has fueled the fire of hurt and anger for the people involved. Ask the group to stand in a circle and have each person share how they have added to the problem being addressed. Ask them to hold their pencils toward the circle's center, eventually touching the other pencils. Explain how each of their words fueled the situation. Discuss how a fire grows with more fuel added to it. Now, ask each participant to commit to an action that helps alleviate the situation. As each expresses a solution, have them pull their pencil out of the circle and point out the dwindling of the imagined flames. Unfueled flames eventually die out.

Read the entire chapter that contains this passage. Reflect and pray about its meaning. _____

_____

- What insights are there when considering the historical or situational context? _____

_____

- What speaks to you directly? _____

_____

- How does it apply to your message? _____

_____

- What personal story will you describe to help others apply this truth?_____

_____

_____

- What type of preparation might you need to use the props effectively? _____

_____

72. Scripture: Ephesians 6:10–18

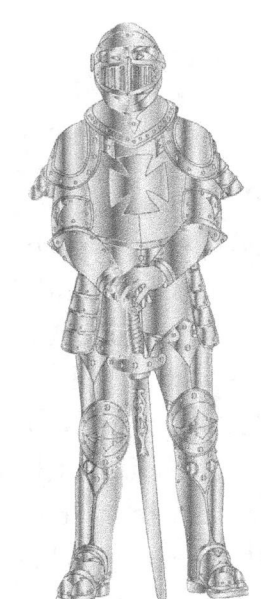

- **Theme:** The Armor of Christ

- **Visual Aids:** Use a child's knight costume with a helmet, shield, sword, breastplate, belt with a large buckle, hiking shoes, and your hands for prayer.

- **Application:** Hold up each piece of armor as you describe its purpose as explained in the Scripture. And don't forget to add prayer as a piece of armor.

Read the entire chapter that contains this passage. Reflect and pray about its meaning. _____

_____

- What insights are there when considering the historical or situational context? _____

_____

- What speaks to you directly? _____

_____

- How does it apply to your message? _____

_____

- What personal story will you describe to help others apply this truth?_____

_____

_____

- What type of preparation might you need to use the props effectively? _____

_____

_____

73. Scripture: Philippians 2:3-8

- **Theme:** Comparison

- **Visual Aids:** Use three glass measuring cups with scale markings. Fill two with varied amounts and the third (the biggest, if possible) to the brim.

- **Application:** Picture your gifts, aptitudes, and resources blended into a measuring cup. Each of us has a different amount. Our temptation is to use the lines and markings to compare ourselves to others. But Jesus, whose measuring cup is full to the brim, emptied Himself and poured His life out on the cross. He invites us to follow His example and humbly focus on the spout, not the lines. When we tip our measuring cups, the lines become irrelevant.

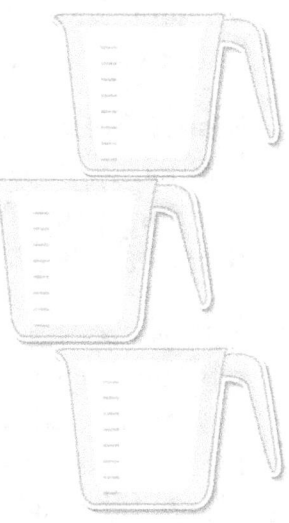

Image: vecteezy.com

- **Contributor:** Shannon Popkin

Read the entire chapter that contains this passage. Reflect and pray about its meaning. _____

_____

- What insights are there when considering the historical or situational context? _____

_____

- What speaks to you directly? _____

_____

- How does it apply to your message? _____

_____

- What personal story will you describe to help others apply this truth?_____

_____

_____

- What type of preparation might you need to use the props effectively? _____

_____

74. Scripture: Philippians 4:4–8

- **Theme:** Take Your Worries and Anxieties to God with Prayer and Thanksgiving

- **Visual Aids:** Use a backpack with either rocks or items symbolizing specific worries (family picture, car keys, cooking pan, Bible, child-sized clothing, an alcohol bottle, a wallet or checkbook, and prescriptions).

- **Application:** Take out each item, name the worry, and reframe it positively. It might be through gratitude, praise, lessons learned, or other ways. This exercise reframes the focus on the faithfulness of God and how He reveals Himself through difficult times.

Read the entire chapter that contains this passage. Reflect and pray about its meaning. _____

_____

- What insights are there when considering the historical or situational context? _____

_____

- What speaks to you directly? _____

_____

- How does it apply to your message? _____

_____

- What personal story will you describe to help others apply this truth?_____

_____

_____

- What type of preparation might you need to use the props effectively? _____

_____

_____

75. Scripture: Philippians 4:6

- **Theme:** Anxiety

- **Visual Aid:** Use a string tied in knots. Label each knot with a concern that causes stress. You can even tie these as you speak of your challenges.

- **Application:** As your message describes how God helped you overcome these challenges with prayer and thanksgiving, untie each knot.

Read the entire chapter that contains this passage. Reflect and pray about its meaning. _____

_____

- What insights are there when considering the historical or situational context? _____

_____

- What speaks to you directly? _____

_____

- How does it apply to your message? _____

_____

- What personal story will you describe to help others apply this truth?_____

_____

_____

- What type of preparation might you need to use the props effectively? _____

_____

_____

76. Scripture: Philippians 4:8

- **Theme:** Rewriting the Messages, We Listen To

- **Visual Aids:** Use a Bible, a microphone, and a message recorded on a cell phone.

- **Application:** The recorded message represents the messages we listen to in our heads. The microphone represents God's voice reading His Word from the Bible to record over those old messages and acknowledge Him. Instead of fixing our minds on the old messages, God wants us to fix our minds on positive things.

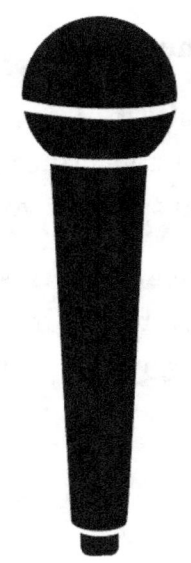

Read the entire chapter that contains this passage. Reflect and pray about its meaning. _____

_____

- What insights are there when considering the historical or situational context? _____

_____

- What speaks to you directly? _____

_____

- How does it apply to your message? _____

_____

- What personal story will you describe to help others apply this truth?_____

_____

_____

- What type of preparation might you need to use the props effectively? _____

_____

_____

77. Scripture: Philippians 4:11–13

Additional Scripture Resource: **James 1:2–4**

- **Theme:** When Life Gives You Lemons

- **Visual Aids:** Use a basket of fresh lemons, sugar, water, and a pitcher of lemonade.

- **Application:** Although lemons are sour, they can make a sweet drink with sugar and water. Use this to explain how to make the best of things by adding the sweetness of God's strength and the support of the Scriptures to carry us through hard times.

- **Contributor:** Julie Pfeifer

Read the entire chapter that contains this passage. Reflect and pray about its meaning. _____

_____

- What insights are there when considering the historical or situational context? _____

_____

- What speaks to you directly? _____

_____

- How does it apply to your message? _____

_____

- What personal story will you describe to help others apply this truth?_____

_____

_____

- What type of preparation might you need to use the props effectively? _____

_____

_____

78. Scripture: Colossians 2:1–8

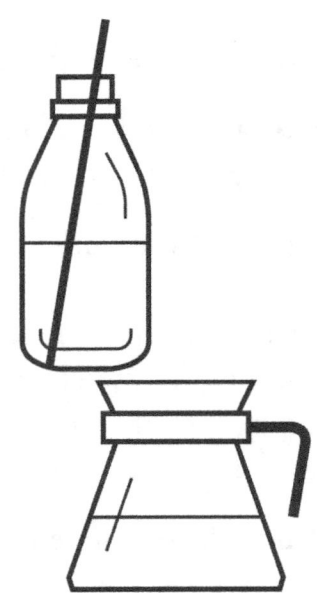

- **Theme:** Vigilance Against False Philosophies

- **Visual Aids:** Use two clear pitchers or vases, a bottle of Gatorade, and a bottle of antifreeze.

- **Application:** Pour the antifreeze into one pitcher and Gatorade into the other. They look similar in color. If you are unaware and accidentally drink the antifreeze, it can harm you and even lead to death. This illustrates that we need to be vigilant against the hollow philosophies of our world or unbiblical concepts. The liquids may look the same, but accidentally drinking the wrong one will severely harm your health, as wrong philosophies can harm your life.

- **Contributor:** Nick Tompkins

Read the entire chapter that contains this passage. Reflect and pray about its meaning. _____

_____

- What insights are there when considering the historical or situational context? _____

_____

- What speaks to you directly? _____

_____

- How does it apply to your message? _____

_____

- What personal story will you describe to help others apply this truth?_____

_____

_____

- What type of preparation might you need to use the props effectively? _____

_____

79. Scripture: Colossians 3:12–14

- **Theme:** Clothing Ourselves in the Attributes of Christ

- **Visual Aids:** Use six banners or sashes and one red shawl or larger sash.

- **Application:** Each banner or sash is labeled with one of the values in verses 12 and 13: compassion, patience, humility, kindness, gentleness, and forgiveness. The large sash or shawl represents love and is used to wrap around all the others. You can drape these on a table or chair or even have volunteers hold them up.

Read the entire chapter that contains this passage. Reflect and pray about its meaning. _____

_____

- What insights are there when considering the historical or situational context? _____

_____

- What speaks to you directly? _____

_____

- How does it apply to your message? _____

_____

- What personal story will you describe to help others apply this truth?_____

_____

_____

- What type of preparation might you need to use the props effectively? _____

_____

_____

80. Scripture: 1 Thessalonians 5:16

- **Theme:** Celebration

- **Visual Aids:** Use helium balloons.

- **Application:** Balloons represent a celebration of any kind. "Heaven can seem so far away. We have a million questions about the logistics of it all and what it will be like. Who's to say it isn't filled with balloons? It is, after all, filled with celebration and love."[18]

- **Contributor:** Bob Goff (used with permission)

Read the entire chapter that contains this passage. Reflect and pray about its meaning. _____

_____

- What insights are there when considering the historical or situational context? _____

_____

- What speaks to you directly? _____

_____

- How does it apply to your message? _____

_____

- What personal story will you describe to help others apply this truth?_____

_____

_____

- What type of preparation might you need to use the props effectively? _____

_____

[18] Bob Goff, *Everybody, Always* (Nashville: Thomas Nelson Inc, 2018).

81. Scripture: 2 Timothy 2:15

- **Theme:** Bible Study

- **Visual Aids:** Use several how-to books, such as books on cooking, home décor, exercise, and hobbies. You will also need a Bible and a Bible study book.

- **Application:** If we study books on how to cook, exercise, fish, and so on, how much more should we study God's Word?

Read the entire chapter that contains this passage. Reflect and pray about its meaning. _____

_____

- What insights are there when considering the historical or situational context? _____

_____

- What speaks to you directly? _____

_____

- How does it apply to your message? _____

_____

- What personal story will you describe to help others apply this truth?_____

_____

_____

- What type of preparation might you need to use the props effectively? _____

_____

_____

82. Scripture: Hebrews 13:7

- **Theme:** Mentoring

- **Visual Aids:** Use a running baton.

- **Application:** Demonstrate passing the baton. We learn from others. We are called to share everything about our faith and to encourage them in theirs, whether they are behind us, ahead of us, or alongside of us. God uses our experiences to minister to others.

- **Contributor:** Kris Howsley King

Read the entire chapter that contains this passage. Reflect and pray about its meaning. _____

_____

- What insights are there when considering the historical or situational context? _____

_____

- What speaks to you directly? _____

_____

- How does it apply to your message? _____

_____

- What personal story will you describe to help others apply this truth?_____

_____

_____

- What type of preparation might you need to use the props effectively? _____

_____

_____

83. Scripture: James 1:2

- **Theme:** Count It All Joy

- **Visual Aids:** Use small sparkly items such as colored floral stones or Hershey's Kisses. You will also need rocks and a large vase.

- **Application:** The rocks represent challenging situations. Put these into the vase as people call them out. Then, ask them to identify some blessings. Add sparkly items to the vase as they name those blessings or joys. Visually seeing the blessings multiply helps you count the joys. Point out how you can see the bright colors better than the rocks. This is the joy amid adversity.

Image: vecteezy.com

Read the entire chapter that contains this passage. Reflect and pray about its meaning. _____

_____

- What insights are there when considering the historical or situational context? _____

_____

- What speaks to you directly? _____

- How does it apply to your message? _____

_____

- What personal story will you describe to help others apply this truth?_____

_____

_____

- What type of preparation might you need to use the props effectively? _____

_____

84. Scripture: James 1:17

- **Theme:** Change Is Hard, but God Never Changes

- **Visual Aid:** Invite each audience member to cross their arms, knees, or ankles.

- **Application:** Ask the audience to look at their arms (knees or ankles) and identify which arm is on top. Now, challenge them to cross their limbs with the opposite limb on top. Ask how it feels. Change is difficult, uncomfortable, and requires focus and, sometimes, help from others. But God is the same and is always with us through those difficult times.

Try this your-self. I have done this with many different groups. Most people are amazed at how different this feels. Ask for a show of hands on how many could feel the difference. Typically, a few say there is no dif-ference. You can easily address this by saying,

We all handle change differently.

Read the entire chapter that contains this passage. Reflect and pray about its meaning. _____

_____

- What insights are there when considering the historical or situational context? _____

_____

- What speaks to you directly? _____

_____

- How does it apply to your message? _____

_____

- What personal story will you describe to help others apply this truth?_____

_____

_____

- What type of preparation might you need to use the props effectively? _____

_____

_____

85. Scripture: Revelation 3:4–19

- **Theme:** A Warning to the Laodiceans to be Either Hot or Cold, Not Lukewarm

- **Visual Aids:** Use gold coins or chains, black fabric, a mortar and pestle, a thermos with hot liquid, a clear glass filled with ice water, and a water bottle or a flat can of soda.

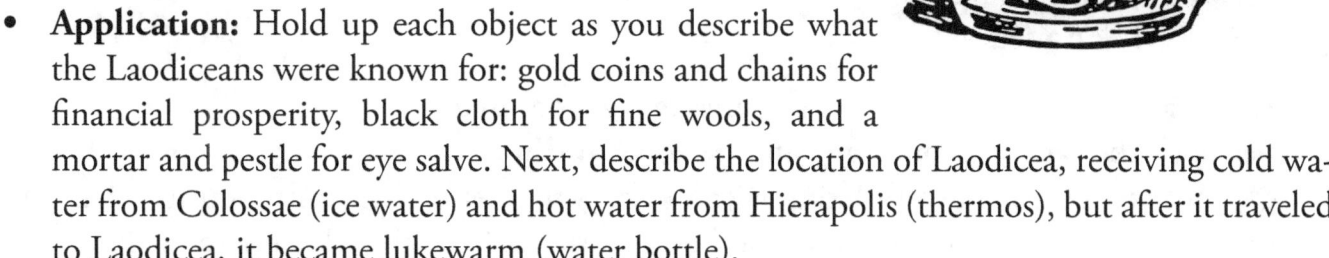

- **Application:** Hold up each object as you describe what the Laodiceans were known for: gold coins and chains for financial prosperity, black cloth for fine wools, and a mortar and pestle for eye salve. Next, describe the location of Laodicea, receiving cold water from Colossae (ice water) and hot water from Hierapolis (thermos), but after it traveled to Laodicea, it became lukewarm (water bottle).

- **Contributor:** Cindy Bultema[19]

Read the entire chapter that contains this passage. Reflect and pray about its meaning. _____

_____

- What insights are there when considering the historical or situational context? _____

_____

- What speaks to you directly? _____

_____

- How does it apply to your message? _____

_____

- What personal story will you describe to help others apply this truth?_____

_____

- What type of preparation might you need to use the props effectively? _____

_____

[19] Cindy Bultema, Red Hot Faith: Lessons from a Lukewarm Church (Grand Rapids: Discovery House, 2014).

86. Scripture: Revelation 3:16

- **Theme:** A Warning to the Laodiceans to Be Either Hot or Cold, Not Lukewarm

- **Visual Aids:** Use three chairs with signs that read as follows:
  1. Hot—Committed
  2. Warm—Compromised
  3. Cold—Confused

- **Application:** Explain that cold represents a confused person; lukewarm, a compromising person; and hot, a committed person. Sit in the seats as you discuss this verse. The compromising chair represents the person who can't decide and follows the easiest path. This is like the lukewarm person in the scripture. They never make a commitment and are easily swayed to change their beliefs and follow the crowd. Jesus knew that it is easier for a confused (cold) person to move to a spirit of commitment (hot) than to convince a compromising (lukewarm) person.

Read the entire chapter that contains this passage. Reflect and pray about its meaning. _____

_____

- What insights are there when considering the historical or situational context? _____

_____

- What speaks to you directly? _____

_____

- How does it apply to your message? _____

_____

- What personal story will you describe to help others apply this truth?_____

_____

- What type of preparation might you need to use the props effectively? _____

_____

87. Scripture: Revelation 3:20

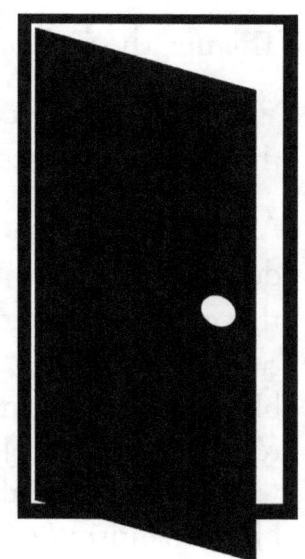

- **Theme:** Standing at the Door and Knocking

- **Visual Aids:** Use a block of wood, a hammer, and a door, or a picture of a door.

- **Application:** Demonstrate different ways of knocking on the wood. Tap with your nails, slap with your hand, knock with your knuckles, and then pound with the hammer. Each way symbolizes the subtle and obvious ways Jesus knocks on our hearts. Point out that the door where Jesus stands does not have a doorknob on His side. We must open the door.

Read the entire chapter that contains this passage. Reflect and pray about its meaning. _____

_____

- What insights are there when considering the historical or situational context? _____

_____

- What speaks to you directly? _____

_____

- How does it apply to your message? _____

_____

- What personal story will you describe to help others apply this truth?_____

_____

_____

- What type of preparation might you need to use the props effectively? _____

_____

_____

88. Lessons with Multiple Scriptures

- **Theme:** The Gift of Grace

- **Visual Aids:** Use colored streamers, balloons, or balls in the colors black, red, white, blue, green, and yellow.

- **Application:** First decide which prop you will use. As you describe each part to the salvation story, hold the object that matches the color that coincides with your explanation.
  black = sin (Romans 3:23)
  red = the blood of Jesus (John 3:16)
  white = purity (Psalm 51:7)
  blue = baptism (2 Corinthians 5:17)
  green = growth (Colossians 1:9–12)
  yellow = light (John 9:5)

Read the entire chapter that contains this passage. Reflect and pray about its meaning. _____

_____

- What insights are there when considering the historical or situational context? _____

_____

- What speaks to you directly? _____

_____

- How does it apply to your message? _____

_____

- What personal story will you describe to help others apply this truth? _____

_____

_____

- What type of preparation might you need to use the props effectively? _____

_____

89. *Lessons with Multiple Scriptures*

- **Theme:** Labels Versus Identity in Christ

- **Visual Aids:** Use large sticky name tags with words such as dumb, ugly, worthless, ashamed, abandoned, etc. written in large print. In addition, prepare name tags with the positive identity words associated with the scriptures you choose to use.

Image: vecteezy.com

- **Application:** This message focuses on our vulnerability to the world's voices that highlight our flawed earthly image, but our identity comes from Christ. As you tell your story, put on the negative name tags. As you describe your transformation in Christ, rip off the negative name tags and replace them with positive ones as you read the related scripture. A few ideas are listed below, and more in the book *Live Full, Walk Free.*[20]
  - accepted (Romans 15:7)
  - beautiful (Song of Songs 4:7)
  - overcomer (1 John 4:4)
  - qualified (Colossians 1:12)
  - chosen (John 15:16)
  - gifted (1 Peter 4:10)

- **Contributor:** Cindy Bultema, *Live Full Walk Free*

Read the entire chapter that contains this passage. Reflect and pray about its meaning. _____

_____

- What insights are there when considering the historical or situational context? _____

_____

- What speaks to you directly? _____

- How does it apply to your message? _____

_____

- What personal story will you describe to help others apply this truth? _____

_____

- What type of preparation might you need to use the props effectively? _____

_____

[20] Cindy Bultema, *Live Full, Walk Free: Set Apart in a Sin-Soaked World* (New York: HarperCollins, 2016).

Chapter 4: Other Creative Ideas

Using Scarves to Interpret Scripture

Using a single long rectangular scarf to read Scripture can add to the effectiveness of the reading. Change the scarf to symbolize the characters. It is essential to be very familiar with your passage and to practice this technique until it is smooth instead of awkward. See the examples below:

90. The Prodigal Son: Luke 15:11–32

1. Father: wear the scarf like a shawl, showing his age.

2. Older son: wear the scarf like a stole over your shoulders, symbolizing a judge.

3. Younger son: wear the scarf tied around your waist like a servant. When he returns, move the scarf over your head, symbolizing shame.

As you read, position yourself by turning in one direction as the father and the other as each of the sons. Make sure you vary your voice with the position to accentuate each character.

In the end, when the father runs to meet the son,
   1. Have the shawl over the son's head.
   2. Then transfer it around the father's shoulders.
   3. When you read the words, "Bring the best robe," change your position and ceremoniously transfer the scarf to the son like a royal robe.

91. Gabriel's Visit to Mary: Luke 1:26–38

1. Gabriel: Drape the scarf over your shoulders to symbolize wings.

2. Mary: Pull the scarf over your head like a hood.

3. Narrator: Hold the scarf in your hand.

92. Joseph Interprets Dreams: Genesis 40:1-23

1. Joseph: Drape the scarf around your shoulders to symbolize a cloak. Even though Joseph does not have his cloak, this is a subliminal sign of the future.

2. Cup Bearer: Fold the scarf over your bent arm like a towel. Your posture is important.

3. Baker: Wrap the scarf around your waist like an apron.

4. Narrator: Hold the scarf in your hand.

Drama

Dress up as a biblical character and dramatize the story in first person. Whether you use a published script or write your own, this method requires memorization and practice. Before you present it to your audience, practice movements, gestures, verbal expressions, and facial expressions. Videotape yourself or practice in front of a person or mirror.

Practical tips for writing your script:

1. What do you know about the characters?

2. What are the cultural influences?

3. What could have been their experiences?

4. What emotions might be demonstrated?

5. How would you portray this? Think- body language, facial expressions, words.

6. What is the message you want the audience to receive?

Costuming

When portraying a character, you can wear a full costume or personify them by using a scarf, hat, jacket, or small props. If you wear hats and jackets for your characters, decide how to display them before and after using them. Some people bring in a rod to hang the hangers. Sometimes, I go behind a screen to change or use chairs to organize my costume pieces and props.

If I change into partial costuming or use scarves, I wear all black. It provides a neutral palette. Suppose the character requires an entire outfit; decide how you will enter and exit. A dress rehearsal is recommended to confirm that there are no issues. Avoiding modern distractions such as jewelry or brightly painted nails is vital.

Preparation:

1. Practice at home.

2. Memorize your script. I was inspired to do this type of ministry after seeing a character in a beautiful costume enter the stage and pull out index cards as she read her script.

3. Videotape yourself and critique it.

4. Visit the venue a day ahead or earlier to practice.

5. Walk through your movements in space. Does anything need to be moved? Are there steps or cords that could interfere?

6. Decide how you will enter and exit.

7. Inquire about a room where you can change.

8. Do a sound check with a lapel or head microphone.

9. Before you dress in your costume, place the microphone so the costume does not interfere.

10. Practice, practice, practice.

Audience Involvement

"To be effective, it is vital to connect as soon as possible with your audience. This starts as soon as the attendees arrive. Circulate and introduce yourself as the speaker. This demonstrates that you're interested in them, relatable, and confident."
—Sue Heimer (contributor)

Specific ideas for audience involvement:

- Have the audience repeat a phrase to emphasize a central point. I have seen many speakers use this effectively.

- Throw a beach ball into the audience, increasing attention and engagement. It can be used to encourage participants to call out answers.

- Tell a story and divide the audience into sections with simple responses for parts of the story. Marnie Swedberg has a specific example on the next page in her submission, "Peace Amid Pressure."

- Start a familiar scripture and have the audience finish it for you or recite it with you.

- Begin a familiar song, TV theme song, or commercial jingle and have the audience complete it. If you use this, it's important to know your audience and use the songs that are a part of their experience: age, interests, culture, etc. (Contributor: Tammy Whitehurst)

Ask the audience to raise their hands or shake keys in response to a yes or no question. Some speakers have audience members stand and sit to respond. Sue Heimer has audience members wave something in the air. She introduces it something like this:
"I would like you to please find something you can wave in the air. This could be a piece of paper or a tissue. We are going to do what my grandma would call a hanky wave." I demonstrate this and then invite them to do a practice hanky wave. This relaxes the women, who may be timid about getting something out. They quickly find something when they see everyone else doing a practice wave. I explain that I will ask a series of questions, and if they can relate, I want them to give me a vigorous hanky wave.

- **Contributor:** Sue Heimer

An Engaging Audience Participation Game

- **Theme:** Peace Amidst Pressure

- **Visual Aid:** Use a large Jenga game.

- **Application:** Set up a Jenga game on the stage. Ask for two volunteers who already know how to play and love the game. As they come up, instruct the audience that the women on the left side of the room (team one) will be shouting out one phrase while the women on the other side (team two) shout another phrase at your direction (like a choir director).

- Phrases for team one:
  "Careful!"
  "It's going to fall!"
  "Oh, no!"

- Phrases for team two:
  "You can't do it!"
  "It's too hard!"
  "This is embarrassing!"

Begin the game in silence. Let the two contestants get a few moves in before you bring in one team at a low (quiet) level. As you move into the game, use your arms like a conductor to increase the volume, ending with both teams at a frantic pitch and yelling simultaneously—end by interviewing the candidates about how it felt.

- **Contributor:** Marnie Swedberg

Increase the Impact of Your Prop

Integrating your prop into multiple parts of your message or lesson increases its impact. The following are examples of increasing the visibility of your prop. I have described using a cup in one of my messages, Molded by the Master.

1. Introduction—At the beginning of your message, introduce your prop.
    • The cup symbolizes the difference between our outer appearance and inner self. Different cups are displayed and described. For example, A beautiful cup may contain coffee grounds, and a plain cup may contain beautiful jewels.

2. Highlight the scripture.
    • One of the verses used in my cup theme is Ephesians 2:10 (page 79). I use the same cups from the introduction to emphasize this verse.

3. Pray about how the prop can be used during a high-impact moment.
    • I share a challenging period in my life and describe feeling broken. At that point, I smash the cup in the bag on a board. Ensure the cup is in a bag, and you use a safe surface to hit it. I use a cutting board.

4. Wrap-Up— Decide how the prop can be brought out again to emphasize the focus of your message.
    • To symbolize God's faithfulness, I will put the broken pieces into a clear cup and then fill it with water, described as Jesus' living water.

5. Use the prop to create a thread throughout a presentation at your back table. You can have jewelry items, magnets, or other trinkets created that align with your theme or your props.
    • For example, I could sell coffee cups inscribed with Ephesians 2:10 at my table.

Contributors: Lisa Saruga and Peg Arnold

Chapter 5: But Wait! There's More!

Acronyms and Acrostics

Acronyms and acrostics are helpful tools to provide a takeaway for your audience. These are created by choosing a word and giving meaning to each letter in the word. It is referred to as a mnemonic because it helps people remember the main points of your message. Acronyms usually have one word associated with each letter; however, acrostics have a phrase beginning with a specific letter.

Listed below are some possible visual aids to use with acronyms:

- Create posters with the words written on them and hold them up when introducing each word.

- Handouts: Create a PowerPoint slide and a matching handout that attendees can take home. This can also be a lead magnet for collecting email addresses.

- Blow-up letters: Bring small blow-up letters that match your acronym. These are available in different colors at a dollar store. Before the message, I choose audience members to hold up the letters when I give the signal. This creates curiosity and opportunities for participation. I have also worked with the event coordinator to have them displayed on stage.

- Examples of acronyms and acrostics include the following:

The Parts of Prayer

Idea One: <u>A.C.T.S.</u>

A: Adoration, **C:** Confession, **T:** Thanksgiving, **S:** Supplication

Idea Two: <u>P.R.A.Y.</u>

P: Praise, **R:** Repent, **A:** Ask, **Y:** Yield

The Traits of Philippians 4:8 (PLANTER)

P: Pure and Praiseworthy, **L:** Lovely, **A:** Admirable, **N:** Noble, **T:** True and Trustworthy **E:** Excellent, **R:** Right

A Christmas Devotion (PRESENT)

P: Pause and pray, **R:** Rejoice, **E:** Embrace, **S:** Surrender the "shoulds," **E:** Emphasize the essentials, **N:** Nurture yourself, **T:** Thank God and others

Limiting Beliefs (P-O-S-T-I-T-N-O-T-E-S)

P: Powerful, **O:** Observations, **S:** Stuck, **T:** To, **I:** Ideas, **T:** That **N:** Never, **O:** Offer, **T:** The, **E:** Eves (Eve representing women), **S:** Solutions or Success in life

- **Visual Aids:** Use Post-it Notes.

- **Application**: Circles, hearts, squares, and all colors work well in teaching and speaking. For example, with limiting beliefs, women often say, "I cannot do that. I am too old. I am not techy. It's not perfect. I am not good enough." You, as the speaker, can stick these Post-it Notes one by one on your cheek, body, or head. You can place them on a board or ask a volunteer from the audience to be your model.

Contributor: Darlene Larson

"Go Eat Popcorn."

A memorization phrase for the New Testament epistles (letters)

Go: Galatians, **Eat:** Ephesians, **Pop:** Philippians, **Corn:** Colossians

Awareness (TEAL)

T: Talk, **E:** Explore, **A:** Act, **L:** Legislate

(This example addresses sexual assault awareness but could be adapted to any cause that uses a colored ribbon.)

- **Visual Aid:** Use an oversized, teal-colored puffer jacket.

- **Application:** Teal is the awareness color for sexual assault. It's essential to wear a huge teal puffer coat, making it very dramatic and outrageous. Explain that we can wear a little teal ribbon to show that we are aware of sexual assault, but it takes "big TEAL" action to affect meaningful change.

Here are action steps using the acrostic TEAL:

T - Talk to someone to raise awareness.

E - Explore local resources and consider volunteering or donating.

A - Act out your values; be the example.

L - Legislation: vote and write to your legislators.

Contributor: Lisa Saruga

Strength Through Heartbreak (STRENGTH)

S - Seek God and invite Him into your pain.

T - Tearfully allow yourself time to grieve and process the emotions.

R - Replace your finite view with God's infinite perspective.

E - Embrace God's character development in the midst of chaos.

N - Never lose sight of God's grace.

G - Give praise to God even as your heart breaks.

T - Trust that God is good when your mind is doubting and you don't understand.

H - Honestly, share your story and help another hurting heart.

Contributor: Jodi Snowdon[21]

---

[21]Jodi Snowdon, Depth: Growing Through Heartbreak to Strength (Enumclaw, WA: Redemption Press, 2022).

Sticky Statements

Sticky statements summarize ideas from your message. They are short and easy-to-remember sentences or phrases. They can be a call to action, a reminder of one of your essential points, or an encouragement. Sometimes, they rhyme. Sometimes, they use alliteration, creating a phrase where each word starts with the same sound. The Heath Brothers researched the effectiveness of sticky ideas in increasing the retention of a message or an idea.[22]

Mary Snyder teaches her speakers in her Activate course to use sticky statements as an easy-to-remember summary of a central point. Two of Mary's examples are as follows:

- **Her success is not your failure.** It's a turn of phrase that makes this sticky. This statement is built around a message of building up sisters in ministry. We are called to cheer each other on, and cheer for her when she gets the speaking gig or the book deal. Her success doesn't mean you don't get to succeed also; it just means it's her turn.

- **Forward-Focused Faith.** The alliteration is sticky. The statement is built around a message of forging on and marching forward (based on Philippians 3:13–14).

Contributor: Mary Snyder (used by permission)

Here are a couple of sticky statements I use in some of my messages.

"Our mistakes don't define us; through their stories, God refines us." This is part of a message focusing on how God uses our stories for His glory.

"God doesn't just glue our broken pieces together; He recreates something new." This comes from a message called "Strength in the Joys and Challenges."

---

[22]Chip Heath and Dan Heath, *Made to Stick: Why Some Ideas Survive and Others Die* (New York: Random House, 2007). 104.

Storytelling

Storytelling is another multimodal method because you connect to your audience by engaging their imaginations and emotions by creating a vivid picture using words. Stories can be inspiring, engaging, and thought-provoking and provide a foundation for an instant connection between you and the audience.

Mary Snyder says, "Stories connect, and data can bore." (used with permission)

I say there is a time for stories and a time for teaching with facts. Remember, having a graph or chart helps when sharing facts and figures.

Debra Weller says, "Storytellers engage their audience with eye contact, voice variations, and cadence. By listening to the stories of others, we can connect through emotions and the spirit." (used with permission)

One of the questions in the "Bringing Scripture to Life" section asks you to apply a personal story. Stories are an impactful way to connect with your audience.

Some of the master storytellers who have contributed or permitted me to use their ideas are Bob Goff, Carol Kent, Tammy Whitehurst, Robyn Dykstra, Debra Weller, and Mary Snyder. There are many others, like Garrison Keiller and Paul Harvey. Observing a storyteller is one way to learn. Additionally, there are courses you can take to hone your skills.

Chapter 6: Delivery and Preparation

Tone, inflection, timing, volume, pacing—everything you do with your voice communicates something and has the potential to help you connect to or disconnect from others when you speak.
—John C. Maxwell, *Everyone Communicates, Few Connect*

Using Props

Preparation

There are many ways to integrate visuals into your presentation. Below are a few helpful hints to make your visual aids impactful.

1. When you have decided on your visual aids, include reminders or prompts where and when to use them in your script.

2. Make sure the objects are large enough for your presentation venue. Venues with video screens help with this.

3. Practice using them, including placement, timing, and speaking.

4. Consider the stage layout. Will you need a table, a chair, or a tablecloth? If there is a table, I always use a black tablecloth, and I carry one with me with me.

5. Where are the visuals in relation to the lectern? Get to your venue early enough to coordinate the setup, organize your objects, and practice. I always use a music stand instead of a lectern because it gives me complete access to the props.

6. Be aware of your eye contact while using visuals. It's essential to connect with the audience, not the visual aid.

7. Consider the microphone. It is challenging to manage props and a handheld microphone. Options that free your hands are a lapel mike, a mike on a stand, and a head mike. I prefer using a head microphone.

8. Practice, practice, practice.

Power Point

A two-dimensional PowerPoint presentation is the most popular visual aid for enhancing your message. However, adding three-dimensional objects engages more areas of the brain, increasing the impact of your message.

PowerPoint is an excellent tool for sharing maps, diagrams, and charts, such as when speaking of Paul's or your travels or studying scriptures like Ezekiel 40–41, which describes the temple. Using maps and diagrams significantly improves your audience's understanding.

Robyn Dykstra, the creator of the Christian Speakers Boot Camp, has contributed and used the following points. (Used with permission)

1. PowerPoint slides are not intended to be your teleprompter.

2. They have one purpose: to enhance the audience's experience of your presentation.

3. When you use slides as part of your presentation, follow these guidelines:

   a. Keep your slides simple, with a minimum number of words on each slide.

   b. Follow the rule of three: three words per bullet and no more than three bullet points per slide.

   c. Lean on pictures, not text, to carry your point.

   d. If you do use text, use large, easy-to-read fonts.

      i. Give each slide a single message.

      ii. Rely on bullet points, not full sentences, unless it's a quote or Scripture.

Ensure you own the images in your presentation or have permission to use them.

Don't stare at the screen, constantly turning your back to the audience.

Illuminate the slide only while you are talking about it. Once you transition away from the slide's content, go to a blank screen with your logo or the logo of the event on it.

Please do not leave the slides up after you have discussed the material on them. This will keep the audience's attention on you.

PowerPoint slides are a terrific way to enhance your talk when appropriately used but can be a huge distraction when they're not.

Contributor: Robyn Dykstra

Verbal Techniques

Using stories and facts mixed with your teaching will keep audiences engaged, but it's not just WHAT you say; it's HOW you say it.

"According to body language experts, the percentage of nonverbal communication we use to communicate with one another is around 60% to 65%."[23] Nonverbal communication includes your voice inflections, facial expressions, and gestures.

After laboring to research and write a brilliant presentation, deliver it using vocal variety and watch the audience lean in, listen intently, and take action.

Every word, gesture, facial expression, and tonal inflection leads the audience to the outcome you hope for—OR distracts them from it. Using vocal variety keeps your audience engaged and your message memorable.

Volume: Good vocal variety is critical to your message. It requires varying your volume during a speech. Use an average conversational volume interspersed with forceful, commanding accentuations with soft, quiet tones.

Pitch and Expression: Your expression and tone should match the message's emotion, mood, and content.

Pace: Varying your speaking pace means speeding up and slowing down to match your emotions and emphasize specific portions.

Pause: The phrase "the power of the pause." means that strategic pauses keep your listener tuned in to your message.

Lipstick: Contrasting lipstick is helpful because it accentuates your mouth as you speak. This is especially important in small groups where you might not be amplified.

Contributor: Robyn Dykstra

---

[23] Phil Taylor, "Your Guide to Understanding Body Language," Body Language Matters.

Conclusion

Perhaps you have always believed that visual aids are only helpful with children. I want to challenge you. As a speaker, teacher, or preacher, experiment with integrating a visual aid or prop into your next presentation. As a writer, place the physical object you are trying to describe next to your computer while writing. You may be surprised how this approach stimulates your brain and enhances your descriptions.

Remember, visual aids and props that are used well enhance the message and activate the memory. The possibilities are endless. Perhaps this resource has triggered new ideas for your message. Often, a person will reach out to me a year later about a message. They usually describe the drama or visuals that made it memorable. I pray that your ministry is blessed as you develop your unique style message and lessons that will captivate your audiences and make your message unforgettable.

God has given you a gift and desires your message to engage and captivate your audience, moving them closer in their walk with Him. Why not try a prop next time and see what He can do?

Have fun, be creative, and pray!

Scripture Reference Index

Only the first verse is listed of longer sections

Topic Index

Contributors

Angie Baughman is the founder of Steady On ministries and creator of the Step By Step Bible study method. She teaches finding God's faithfulness in the painful places of our lives. https://linktr.ee/livesteadyon

Marie Beck is on the pastoral staff at Mill City Church. Her passions are strategic church leadership, women's ministry, and creating opportunities for people to experience freedom and belovedness through small-group connections.

Cindy Bultema is a popular Bible teacher, conference speaker, and author, but her number-one ministry is being a wife to her husband and a mom to her four kids. She loves to encourage other women and help them experience the fullness of life that Jesus offers. https://www.cindybultema.com/

Kim Cusimano is a wife, mother of four, special needs parent, and writer! She loves to write and share with others, especially caregivers, about the joy and hope found in Jesus! Fulljoyministries.com

Robyn Dykstra is a popular Christian speaker and creator of Christian Speakers Boot Camp, a program that equips aspiring and established speakers to tell their story and teach God's Word with excellence. www.robyndykstra.com

Bob Goff is a charismatic author, speaker, coach, and dreamer. He has authored many books, including the ones quoted in this resource: *Love Does* and *Everybody, Always*. https://www.bobgoff.com/

Linda Y. Hammond, forgiven Christ-follower, wife, mother, grandmother, writer, and speaker, encourages the brokenhearted to experience renewal through Jesus Christ. Formerly a senior pastor's administrative assistant, she now co-leads the Christian Writers Workshop in Waco, Texas. lyhammond86@gmail.com

Jackie Hayden is a speaker, author, mentor, and pastor's wife. As a pastor's wife, she loves to pour encouragement over women on their journey of disappointment and hurts. "Just when the caterpillar thought the world was over, it became a butterfly." jackiehaydenspeaks.com

SueAnn Heimer is a speaker, counselor, author, and teacher. www.sueheimer.com

Amy Robnik Joob is an award-winning author, speaker, coach, and model turned advocate. She is the author of *Model Behavior: Make Your Career Path Your Calling* and a 40-day prayer journal titled *Unstuck: Step into the New.* Married to Eric for 25 years and mom to Arianna and Ashton, Amy lives in the suburbs of Chicago. AmyJoob@yahoo.com

Carol Kent is a best-selling author and speaker. She's the founder of the Speak Up Conference for writers and speakers, along with the nonprofit organization Speak Up for Hope. www.speakupministries.com

Kris Howsley King is a colorful and chatty author, speaker, life coach, and lover of stories who enjoys empowering and equipping women to live their God-given purpose with joy! https://krishowsleyking.com/

Nicole Langman is a Canadian author, speaker, and clinical therapist. She helps women recover from the unthinkable, stand in courage, and reclaim the truth of who they are in Jesus. www.nicolelangman.com @nicole_langman_officialprofile

Darlene Larson is an author, inspirational speaker, and Grief-loss and Life Purpose Coach®. As the latter, she passionately coaches women to recycle their pain to purpose. www.Heartswithapurpose.com

Amberly Neese is a featured speaker, emcee, and comedian for the Aspire Women's Events and Marriage Date Night, two popular Christian national tours. She and her husband have two adult children and live in Prescott, Arizona. https://amberlyneese.com/

Julie Pfeifer created Loving Christ Ministries to support ministry leaders with ready-to-use resources so their focus can be on building relationships with God and others. Julie and her husband live in Missouri, where they love family, camping, and walking their dogs. julie@lovingchristministries.com

Shannon Popkin invites you to drink deeply of God's story and live like it's true. Shannon has been featured on Revive Our Hearts, P31, FamilyLife, and TGC. Her books include *Comparison Girl* and *Control Girl*, and she hosts the *Live Like It's True* podcast. comparisongirl.com

Jennifer Sakata is a gifted communicator, residing at the corner of real grace and real life. Her winsome joy motivates people to slow down and live a kinder, gentler, more grace-filled life. www.JenniferSakata.com

Lisa Saruga is an LPC and EMDR therapist. As an author and speaker, she breaks down barriers to justice and restoration, demonstrating that faith makes healing possible. Lisa advocates at state and national levels to end sexual violence. LisaSaruga.com

Jill Savage is a speaker, author, podcaster, and coach. She and her husband, Mark, have a thriving marriage ministry. Jillsavage.org

Jodi Snowdon is an author, podcaster, and speaker who helps women grow deeper in their faith and stronger in their relationships. Through God's strength, she emerged from miscarriage, divorce, and losing a dear friend to cancer to help women everywhere experience hope, joy, and purpose through life's unexpected storms. jodisnowdon.com

Mary Snyder coaches speakers looking to move forward in their career and create messages that make a difference. Marysnyder.com

Aaron Stern is the lead pastor of Mill City Church in Fort Collins, Colorado (millcitychurch.org). He is the author of *What's Your Secret: Freedom Through Confession.* He and his wife, Jossie, have four boys.

Marnie Swedberg is someone whom godly women worldwide look to for coaching, connections, and collaboration. As a keynote speaker at Christian Women Conferences, Marnie circumnavigates the globe online and in-person, bringing perspective transformation, deep spiritual healing, and hope, helping women reach women for Christ. Contact her at www.womenspeakers.com/united-states/saint-petersburg/speaker/marnie -swedberg

Carol Tetzlaff is an author, speaker, and associate publisher at Redemption Press. She is passionate about making the Word of God approachable as she invites you into His story. caroltetzlaff.com

Nick Tompkins has been in pastoral ministry since 2005 and is passionate about the design and potential of the church. He is married to his best friend, Hilary, and they have four vibrant, wonderful children.

Debra Weller is an experienced educator and professional storyteller. She is a creative performance artist with more than forty years of experience using storytelling to engage audiences. Debteller136@gmail.com

Tammy Whitehurst is fast-paced, funny, and relatable. She has been described as a "hoot with a capital H!" She tickles the funny bone and touches the soul. TammyWhitehurst.com

Author Biography

Peg Arnold is a national speaker, award-winning author, and drama queen for Jesus. As a dynamic retreat speaker, she loves to inspire, encourage, and equip others to embrace God's love and develop their God-given gifts. She has used a multi-modal approach to her messages and lessons for over forty years. Whether as a teacher, counselor, worship leader, women's ministry leader, author, dramatist, or speaker, Peg has experienced the benefits of this approach and, thus, wanted to create a resource that would benefit and add value to other speakers and teachers in their presentations and messages. There are more than one hundred resources in this book, including contributions from more than twenty-five national and international speakers.

With a master's in counseling, Peg has over twenty-five years of experience working with middle and high school students, families, and staff. She is a retired National Board-Certified Professional School Counselor who developed, modeled, and taught continuing education courses focusing on multi modal learning techniques at the local, state, and national levels.

Her personal publications have included her 2022 Oasis award-winning book, *Devotions for the Distracted Heart,* plus numerous articles, devotions, and stories. These can be found in *Chicken Soup for the Soul, You Version, The Upper Room,* online magazines, several Amazon best-selling anthologies, and her online devotions.

Peg is a wife, mom, and her favorite role is nana to her eight grandchildren. She grew up in Michigan, raised her family in Maryland, and now resides in Colorado.

Find out more at pegarnold.org. Contact her at info@pegarnold.org.